Foreword

Welcome to the T50 Trail guide book which pa [...]
fascinating past, magnificent open spaces and [...]
along the way where people can refuel and ta [...]

Its physical boundaries link Ironbridge in the sou [...] *, Limeshall*
Hill in the north and Granville Country Park in [...] *but the spirit of the trail*
reaches far deeper into the hearts of our communities. It's become a focus of
fundraising for worthy causes, it creates memories for family days out, a trail for
running groups and a new route for hundreds of walkers from around the UK who
spread the story of the trail and help our borough prosper,as well as an opportunity
to positively contribute to the health and well-being of the people in the borough.

I wanted to extend a huge 'thank you' to the many passionate volunteers who made
the trail and this guide book possible. Through their passion, the legacy of Telford's
50th birthday is being kept alive and continues to make positive contributions to
the lives of people in Telford and Wrekin.

Cllr Shaun Davies, Leader Telford & Wrekin Council

The Telford T50 Trail is special for many reasons. It celebrates 50 years of the New
Town. Circling the boundary of the town it takes in a variety of splendid landscapes,
viewpoints and places of interest. It links the people of Telford with their local green
spaces. It will benefit the local economy, encouraging people to visit a splendid
walking area which tends, wrongly, to be overlooked. Wellington, a Walkers Are
Welcome town on the route, sets a fine example in offering a warm welcome to
walkers.

The trail shows the value of investing in the public-path network, to enable people
to enjoy their natural surroundings whether on a short local walk or a longer stretch.
The creation of this route has been an excellent example of co-operation to achieve
a milestone. The Ramblers, Walkers Are Welcome, The Long Distance Walkers
Association, Telford & Wrekin Council, parish councils, businesses and local people
collaborated to identify, waymark, clear and promote this fabulous path in time
for the fiftieth anniversary.

It is a splendid and permanent reminder of the celebrations of Telford's 50 years.
Get out and enjoy it!

Kate Ashbrook, Chair, Ramblers GB

Walkers' Reviews of The Telford T50 50 Mile Trail

The route is excellent, with a mix of road, paths, fields and hills, well marked and easy to follow. Great to complete in smaller sections or go for the full 50 miles in one go. Tink B

Inspiring. Great views and places. Poonam M

Fantastic route, takes you through places that I never knew existed. I stopped off on my run a few times to take in the scenery and wildlife (deer, badgers, bats, foxes). Matthew A

It's brilliant. The bright pink way makers are easy to spot & you can dip in & out at certain points. Emma S

Great to see so many different types of historical interests. Very varied terrain and lots of photographic opportunities. Thoroughly enjoyed the Trail. Derek H

Walked the whole route. Can also be walked in small sections as there are several loops and it bisects existing waymarked paths such as the Silkin Way and Shropshire Way. Well waymarked. I was so taken with the area that I have planned a weekend based at Ironbridge which will take in part of the Trail and The Wrekin. Helen Frankwell Strider Magazine.

This is such a fabulous local resource. Paul Shuttleworth BBC Radio Shropshire

What a wonderful legacy to leave as part of the Telford 50th Anniversary Celebrations. Looking forward to working my way around it and meeting the many visitors and locals that it will attract.. Paul K

Fantastic trail …. easy to dip in and out of, and close to public transport links, try a section and discover some of Telford's well known and lesser known green spaces! Drew W

Really enjoying doing the stages of this walk, as Ironbridge is my home town, I am re-visiting places and discovering new ones! Fab. Jen B

Surprisingly green for an urban trail, and a good few hills. Ian John D

So many green spaces still left to roam in Telford. Sue G

It was an amazing experience, The Ercall was also a challenge after The Wrekin, who put those hills in The Ercall??? but well worth it! Jemma G

Had company on the trail by Limekiln Pool today! (Videoed a fallow deer herd). Lindsay BJ

A lovely walk in Apley Woods - so peaceful and beautiful. Love Wellington

11 of us walked the full trail … we were from various parts of the country including Norfolk and Suffolk. I think I speak for everyone in saying we enjoyed it …. a lovely area and I for one will be back. Michelle A

The Telford T50 50 Mile Trail Walking Guide

Anne Suffolk

Editorial team and stage route descriptions:

Eve Clevenger, Jim Cox, Paula Doherty, Pam Hill, Dag Saunders, Anne Suffolk, Naomi Wrighton

Contents

The notional start point is the large trail information board near Telford Town Park Information Centre, as it is a circular trail, you can start anywhere that suits you. Photo: Derek Houghton

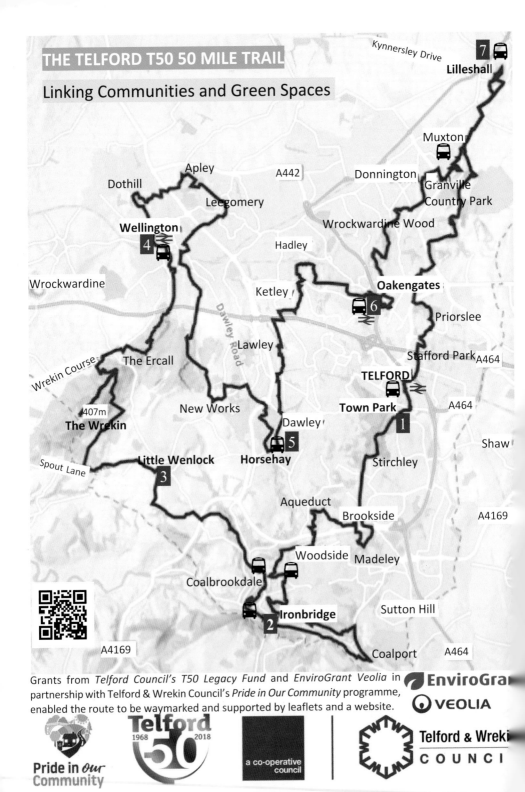

THE TELFORD T50 50 MILE TRAIL

Linking Communities and Green Spaces

Kynnersley Drive

7 **Lilleshall**

Muxton

Apley

Dothill

A442

Donnington

Granville Country Park

Leegomery

Wrockwardine Wood

Wellington

4

Hadley

Oakengates

Wrockwardine

Ketley

Priorslee

6

Dawley Road

Stafford Park A464

The Ercall

Lawley

TELFORD

Wrekin Course

A464

407m

New Works

Town Park

The Wrekin

Dawley

1

Shaw

Spout Lane

Little Wenlock

5

Horsehay

Stirchley

3

Aqueduct

Brookside

A4169

Woodside **Madeley**

Coalbrookdale

Sutton Hill

2 **Ironbridge**

A4169

Coalport

A464

Grants from *Telford Council's T50 Legacy Fund* and *EnviroGrant Veolia* in partnership with Telford & Wrekin Council's *Pride in Our Community* programme, enabled the route to be waymarked and supported by leaflets and a website.

EnviroGra

VEOLIA

Pride in our Community

Telford 1968 50 2018

a co-operative council

Telford & Wreki COUNCI

Welcome to the Telford T50 50 Mile Trail

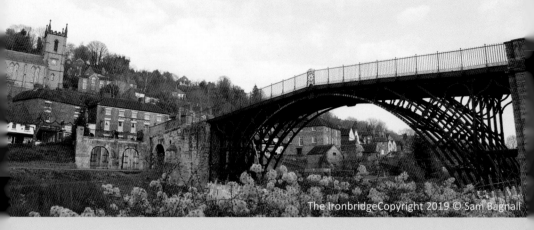

The IronbridgeCopyright 2019 © Sam Bagnall

This new 50 mile circular walking route was created in 2018 to celebrate Telford's 50th anniversary as a New Town. It uses existing footpaths, tracks and quiet roads to form one continuous trail through the many different communities, beautiful green spaces and important heritage sites that make Telford special. The route is waymarked throughout with a magenta 'Telford 50th Anniversary' logo.

The Telford T50 50 Mile Trail showcases local parks, nature reserves, woods, pools and open spaces. It features our history and rich industrial heritage. The route has been designed to go through as many areas of Telford as possible and to be easily accessible by public transport. It is possible to create walks of any length, returning to your starting point by bus or local train. We hope people will want to explore this wonderful new route by starting from the green space closest to where they live.

The Trail begins at the large Trail Information Board in Telford Town Park, goes down to the World Heritage Site at Coalport, Ironbridge and Coalbrookdale, then on through Little Wenlock to The Wrekin, that marvellous Shropshire landmark. It then continues over The Ercall nature reserve through Wellington, Horsehay and Oakengates to Lilleshall, where you can walk to Newport via The Hutchison Way. After Lilleshall it goes through more areas of important industrial heritage, Granville Country Park and back to The Town Centre.

The Trail was opened 16 June 2018 by Kate Ashbrook, Chair of Ramblers GB, General Secretary of the Open Spaces Society and Patron of Walkers Are Welcome, Councillor Raj Mehta, Mayor of Telford & Wrekin and Councillor Shaun Davies, Leader of Telford & Wrekin Council .

PLANNING YOUR TELFORD T50 50 MILE TRAIL WALK

The walk has been divided into seven stages, all of which can be walked at a pace to suit you. The stages between Ironbridge and Wellington may each take a full day if the views, museums, historic places and other attractions are to be fully enjoyed.

There are local buses to all stage start points, and many places in between, with the exception of Little Wenlock. Coalbroodkdale could be an alternative stage point to Little Wenlock for bus users. Trains run fromWellington via Oakengates to Telford Central. For visitors there is ample hotel, bed and breakfast and youth hostel accommodation. For walkers who wish to travel light or take a restful pause, there are many pubs, coffee bars and restaurants, all within a a few minutes of the path and many are on the actual route

Stage 1 – Town Park to Ironbridge 10 miles*

Stage 2 – Ironbridge to Little Wenlock 4 miles*

Stage 3 – Little Wenlock to Wellington 8 miles*

Stage 4 – Wellington to Horsehay 9 miles*

Stage 5 – Horsehay to Oakengates 5 miles*

Stage 6 – Oakengates to Lilleshall 6 miles*

Stage 7 – Lilleshall to Town Park 8 miles*

*The distances for each stage have been rounded up or down by no more than 1/3 mile to give a total distance of 50 miles for the whole trail. The mileages between the numbered sections in the detailed stage route descriptions are a reasonably accurate guide to individual stage lengths when planning your walk. The route is fully waymarked throughout in both directions with a distictive magenta waymark.

This guide book describes the Trail in a CLOCKWISE direction for all sections and stages, including the descriptions of the history and wildlife to be seen along it. We suggest that you walk the various stages in the clockwise direction.

Full directions with measured distances, supporting maps and gpx files (including anticlockwise gpx files and a cycle route that approximates to the Trail) plus links to public transport timetables, facilities on the route, information about other trails that connect with this one, are all available from our website. Bus information was correct at time of going to press Summer 2019. Changes to public transport and walks may occur at short notice. We advise you to check with the transport operators before starting out and follow any official signed diversions in place on paths.

Fifty Miles of History and Heritage under Your Feet

The trail begins and ends in **Telford Town Park** which in 2015 was voted the "UK's Best Park", in the inaugural public competition organised by Fields In Trust. As one might expect there are interesting formal gardens, many water features, adventure playgrounds for all ages from toddlers to teenagers and adults, a splash park, an arena for outdoor events plus a chance for kids to get up close and personal with nursery rhymes and dinosaurs at Wonderland. Any family visitors new to Telford could do worse than explore what is on offer here and most of it is free.

Walking through a World Heritage Site: Telford Town Park to Ironbridge

Telford Town Park is much more than a formal park and playground, it is an important local nature reserve, a preserver of Telford's important industrial heritage, an outdoor museum and it is all much more extensive than most visitors think. **Telford Town Park** is currently 149.6 hectares (370 acres) of open green space in the heart of the town, approximately half of which is designated as a Local Nature Reserve. It was developed in the 1970s by the Telford Development Corporation and transferred to the Local Authority to manage in 1992.

The park is situated on a huge former industrial area including pools and pit mounds, and it contains the impressive **Stirchley Chimney**, 209 feet high, which dominates the skyline to your left as you walk through the park. This is part of the remains of the iron works established in 1790 and closed in 1900. As well as the chimney there are the ruins of two blast furnaces and a rolling mill. You can explore and find out more on the self guided **Heritage Trail** leaflet which can be downloaded from the town park website, or just pick up a copy in the Information Centre adjacent to the start of the Telford T50 50 Mile Trail.

Our Trail intersects in many places with the **South Telford Heritage Trail** and **The Ironbridge Way.** Links to these two trails with their many points of historic interest can be found on our own website.

Just off the Trail, Shropshire's tallest chimney. Well worth a visit, perhaps another day?

The Telford T50 50 Mile Trail starts behind the ruins of an old **C11th Norman Chapel**, originally in Malinsee it was rebuilt here in the park. You skirt **Withy Pool** to your right at the start, the information board about this feature, its history and its wildlife can be found behind the Information Centre. The **Stone Row Cottages** information board is on your right as you leave the pool, these were part of the old **Dark Lane Hamlet** which dated back to 1400.

Ruined Norman chapel

Withy Pool used to be a feeder reservoir for the **Coalport Branch of the Shropshire Canal**, later the pool was used in the iron industry and it is the oldest pool in the Town Park. The canal was built in 1788 to connect the iron industry with the River Severn (a working waterway highway in the past). Very little of the canal remains in the park now, although a little further south, a short section of the original canal waterway may be seen when you walk through Coalport.

As you exit the Town Park you go under an old sandstone bridge, built to carry the newly dug canal over the turnpike road from Bridgnorth to Wellington. This is the remains of the **old aqueduct** which brought water to the canal. The part of Telford called Aqueduct is named after it. Where you turn off the Silkin Way look for the ruins of the old **Madeley Windmill** on your right, it was shown working in 1827 on an old map but disused by the end of the century as steam power took over.

The **Silkin Way** is a long distance footpath which you join for the first couple of miles It follows the line of the canal, later replaced along its length by a passenger railway, and uses old railway tracks. It is an important, very useful north west to south east green corridor, a 14 mile footpath, bridleway and cycleway which starts in Brattor

near Wellington, includes Apley Castle and ends in Coalport. This path is named after Lewis Silkin MP later Lord Silkin, who was instrumental in the Labour Government's 1949 Access to the Countryside Ac and New Towns Act of 1963. When Prime Ministe Jim Callaghan opened it in 1977 it was only designated from the Town Park to Coalport, the northern part was added later. You encounter part of the **Silkin Way** several times along The Telfor T50 50 Mile Trail, look out for the distinctive blac iron wheels at important junctions and milestone:

Silkin Way iron wheel marker

Along your route you will spot many remains of old halts, station platforms, signalling equipment, railway bridges, cuttings, embankments and tunnels which are relics of the disused **London & North Western Railway** line. The best preserved is Stirchley Station renamed **Dawley & Stirchley Station** in July 1923; passenger services began in 1861 and were withdrawn in May 1952. You will encounter this old railway line again on the **Silkin Way**, between Blists Hill Victorian Town and Coalport, where you go through a long **Victorian rail tunnel** (70 yards approximately) towards Coalport. The old brickwork here is very impressive and one can only admire the skills of the old Victorian 'brickies' working by candle and oil lamp. The tunnel ceiling looks a bit low for a train, the reason is the tunnel floor was raised because beneath the **Silkin Way** here lies the **main Telford sewer.**

The Silkin Way follows old rail lines

You can sometimes see interesting rock exposures along the **Silkin Way.** The close proximity of coal, limestone and iron for blast furnaces and clays, for china, bricks and ceramic tiles , was the reason why the industrial revolution started in this region. The rocks were mined by adits, deep mines and some open cast mines in the linked communities of Broseley and Coalbrookdale. Many streams in the Gorge still flow bright orange in colour due to the iron compounds in the water, so after a period of rain, take a closer look at streams and ditches as you pass by. There are prime examples in Short Wood in Stage 4 and by the riverside viewing point of **Bedlam Furnaces** by the **bowl sculptures** near the end of Stage 1.

Iron rich waters

At **Madeley Court** look for the blue plaque on the wall to your right. This 16th-century house was originally built as a grange to the medieval priory at Much Wenlock and the present house was built during the reign of Mary Tudor by Robert Brooke, Speaker of the House of Commons. It was the home of Sir Basil Brooke, 1598 -1646, who set up the first steel furnace in Coalbrookdale. It has many connections to the Reynolds and Darby ironmaster families and it is now a hotel. The pools surrounding the hotel look ornamental but were formerly used as balancing pools for local industry. The bars and restaurant are open to the public and in fine weather you can sit outside. The old **Madeley pit mounds** surrounding this area and the pools are a Local Nature Reserve.

C16th Madeley Court is now a hotel

The beautiful **Dawley Pools** were originally feeder pools for the **Shropshire Can**⸢ used to ferry pig iron. After you exit the pool woodlands you go over the **Lightmoo** **crossing railway line** which was used to serve the local mines, foundries an⸢ brickworks. The line was still in use up to 2017 to serve the **Ironbridge power statio**⸢ and may come back into use as part of the power station site redevelopment. Yc will meet this railway line again after you exit the **Museum of Iron** as you pass und⸢ the viaduct. Just after Lightmoor Crossing you enter Rough Park and follow **Roug** **Park Way** which was the line of an **old tramway from Lightmoor to Coalbrookda**⸢

The T50 descends from Lodge Field towards Madeley from *Hillside* in Ironbridge with many old C19th cottages built along steep narrow lanes and footpaths. Look for a plaque about a famous footballer, well, famous to people who can remember the 1940s and 50s, the first person to win over 100 caps for England, this is *Billy Wright's birthplace*!

Just as you cross the road between these two communities you pass *Dane House*, the last house on the right which was formerly the George and Dragon pub. This is the place where the bodies of the *Nine Men of Madeley* were brought after the pit disaster that claimed their lives and where the first inquest into their deaths took place, as was customary, in the nearest public house to the accident. Four of the nine 'men' were in reality only children, another two were just eighteen. The inquest found that the winding chain that lowered them down the pit shaft had given way. The disaster was blamed on human error. As the man who was said to have had incorrectly attached the chain to the suspension hook and both supervisors were the three adult victims, there was no one left alive to dispute the evidence. The verdict was 'accidental death'. The pit where they worked was up the hill at the top of the road to your left and the pit mound is still there behind a gated housing development. There is a walking trail leaflet you can follow about the disaster and the victims, a link is available via our website.

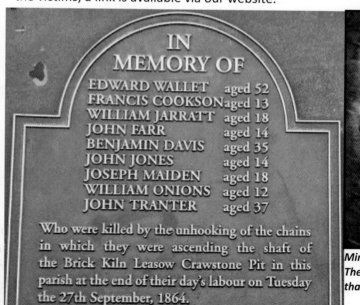

IN MEMORY OF

EDWARD WALLET	aged 52
FRANCIS COOKSON	aged 13
WILLIAM JARRATT	aged 18
JOHN FARR	aged 14
BENJAMIN DAVIS	aged 35
JOHN JONES	aged 14
JOSEPH MAIDEN	aged 18
WILLIAM ONIONS	aged 12
JOHN TRANTER	aged 37

Who were killed by the unhooking of the chains in which they were ascending the shaft of the Brick Kiln Leasow Crawstone Pit in this parish at the end of their day's labour on Tuesday the 27th September, 1864.

Miners riding a lowering chain. The nine men fell 110m, greater than the height of Big Ben.

The mass grave and memorial to the 'nine men' is in St Michael's Churchyard Madeley. Lowering chain and cage failures claimed the lives of 52 men and 'boys 'in C19th Shropshire mines. You pass near the site of Dark Lane pit in Priorslee, where twelve plunged to their deaths in 1862. The eight victims of the 1872 Springwell Pit disaster lie in Holy Trinity Churchyard Dawley. No one was prosecuted for any of these deaths. A great great great nephew of one of the Dawley victims waymarked a lot of our trail.

The **Golden Ball Pub** is one of the oldest in the area dating back to 1728. Wesley Road used to be called Thieve Street, obviously the pub's clientele improved over time, perhaps after the **Wesleyan Chapel and Madeley Wood Wesleyan School** were built and the Methodists got to work on the locals.

The Golden Ball

You go past the workers' entrance to **Blists Hill Victorian Town** in the car park when you cross the road and turn left after exiting **Lloyds Coppice**. To visit the museum continue up the footpath with the museum to the right, for about 400 yards to the main entrance, a 3 -5 hour excursion. Entry to all the museums in the Ironbridge Gorge can be obtained with the *Ironbridge Gorge Museum Pass,* purchased at any museum. More information about this part of the T50 Trail can be found in the *Ironbridge to Blists Hill Victorian Town* trail leaflet published by Severn Gorge Countryside Trust. Free leaflets are available at the Museum of the Gorge, (also check in the leaflet dispensers at the Ironbridge car park and Toll House Visitor Centre as you pass by).

The **Coalport China Works** and the old **Coalport Canal** are on your left, just after you cross the road after leaving the **Silkin Way**. Before you cross the old canal bridge, take a detour of a few yards to take a look at the detailed information boards about the history of Coalport; you can buy an ice cream at the YHA cafe as an excuse to linger while you absorb all the information.

The **Coalport China Museum** on the site of the original factory is well worth a visit but you would need to allocate a few hours to do so. However, it is free to pop in to the museum shop and take a quick look at the information displays, reproductions of old Coalport china and modern pieces on sale there. The huge **Coalport factory pottery kilns,**(see right) are an impressive sight.

As you walk along the last working section of the old **Shropshire Canal** you can see the bottom of the **Hay Inclined Plane** just before crossing over the River Severn at the **Jackfield Memorial Bridge**. Take a moment to leave the path and look under the narrow road bridge for a superb view up the old iron rail lines which transported materials by gravity and steam power up and down the steep incline. This part of the canal did survive in use until about 1894 and the inclined plane was closed in 1907, look out for the information boards and signs about these places as you pass by.

You cross the Severn for the first time at **Jackfield Memorial Bridge.** This bridge is unique, being the only WW1 war memorial footbridge in Britain. The lads who signed up from Coalport and Jackfield lived and worked on opposite sides of the river and had to use a ferry daily, or take a long walk to cross the river, to work or socialise before the war. It was built in 1922 by public subscription, a fitting and practical

tribute to unite the communities of the living who survived, as the lads from these communities had been united in their deaths. The large number of casualties from these two small industrial villages, many related to each other, are listed on a plaque on the middle of the bridge.

After crossing the bridge (look out for kingfishers) pause to look at the **flood door of the Boat pub** showing record flood levels over the years. All the furniture in the pub has to be portable as it must be carried upstairs in a flood emergency so there are no carpets on the tiled floors for obvious reasons. There is a riverside pub garden to enjoy a summertime pint and a snack here.

The **Maws & Co Encaustic Tile Works** to your left as you continue, was the biggest employer in the area between 1883 and its closure in 1969. It is now **Maws Craft Centre** where you are free to wander around and find out more about the history of the factory from the large display boards. There is a cafe and free public toilets on the site. At the end of the factory wall, where you carry straight across into an alleyway, you are on **The Jackfield Tile Trail**. Look for the information boards and the free leaflets in the dispensers or download one from the Internet before your walk.

The trail continues past the back of **The Half Moon** which is another possible place to eat and drink and enjoy riverside views from inside and outside. At the picnic area where you leave the riverside part of the **Jackfield Tile Trail** do pause to admire the beautiful **art work of tiles made by local children** celebrating their enjoyment of the public open spaces, wildlife and history to be found here. There are information boards about the **Jackfield Landslips** which destroyed the village in the 1950s and the **Gorge Stabilisation Works**, an immense and very recent engineering project to prevent it happening again. You can spot the remains of previous attempts to achieve stabilisation and prevent landslides using boiler shells filled with concrete (it didn't work and they were retrieved from the river later!)

Part of children's art work

You will see **Jackfield Church** in front of you from the picnic area viewpoint above the Severn. The church is usually open and you can find the light switch on your right by the door after entering. It is well worth a visit as it shows beautiful examples of artwork made from tiles lovingly crafted by local workers. The altar piece they made was displayed at the Great Exhibition. The colours in the bricks in the exterior walls, doors and windows and roof tiles are all natural, there is colour variation in the local clays used to make the world famous 'Broseley bricks' and 'Broseley tiles'. These differently coloured local bricks and tiles have been used to make beautiful decorative features around doors, windows and on the roof in shades of blue, reds, greys and yellows. Most of the Victorian and early C20th public and industrial buildings you see on the T50 Trail use the same coloured bricks to achieve interesting decorative effects. To your left as you leave Jackfield is the site of the world famous **Craven Dunhill Encaustic Tile Works** built in 1873 now the **Jackfield Tile Museum**. You need a museum pass to get in, however, entry to the museum shop and cafe is free where you can see information boards and modern reproductions of old decorative tiles for sale. Nearly every important Victorian building in the UK displays examples of decorative tiles made in these Ironbridge Gorge factories, as do most floors and fireplaces in middle class homes built in this period.

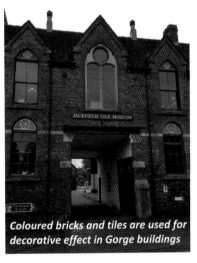

Coloured bricks and tiles are used for decorative effect in Gorge buildings

As you continue your walk you will follow the old track of yet another disused railway. Look out for the old **Jackfield railway crossing gates**, these were reputed to be the widest in Britain. These are all that remains of the **disused Great Western Railway** which ran into Paddington from here. The level crossing gates were rebuilt and restored in 2019. The line continued in the other direction to Shrewsbury and Craven Arms via the old Ironbridge power station site. The Telford T50 50 Mile Trail follows the line as far as the famous iron bridge. **Jackfield station platform** is on your left as you pass the **Black Swan**. If you want a pint, a snack and an excellent view of canoeists trying their skills in the River Severn rapids from the riverside pub garden, there is a path and steps down on your right though the pub's back garden to the pub's welcoming front door. A little further on look for a large information board on your right just after going under a road bridge, this tells you about the origins of the coal and iron works in the Gorge and the **Bedlam Furnaces**. If you leave the path here and walk a few yards towards the river you will get an excellent view of the huge furnace ruins on the opposite river bank plus some interesting modern **'bowl sculptures'**.

The highlight of the end of the first stage of the trail is crossing the **world's first iron bridge**, opened as a toll bridge on New Year's Day in 1781. The bridge is based on the wooden carpentry techniques of the time complete with dovetail joints, which the older ones among us may remember doing in school woodwork classes. Its structure and colour would have resembled a wooden bridge; the original colour was restored in 2018. After crossing the bridge, if you have time, you can walk under it to see it at close quarters and fully appreciate its construction. The **Ironbridge Toll House** has a small free museum about the bridge and the people who made it, including Abraham Darby and 'iron mad' John Wilkinson. There is a small shop too with free information leaflets about local nature and history walking trails and the **Ironbridge Gorge World Heritage Site**, the birthplace of the industrial revolution. On the outside are displayed the old charges for making the crossing (not free for all members of the Royal family as the slightly different script added for Prince Charles' visit shows!) Closed to vehicles in 1934 ,walkers had to pay until 1950 ,when Shropshire Council took over the bridge.

The Iron Bridge
© Glenn Bishton

Eustace Rogers

The **Ironbridge war memorial** used to be in the town square. The soldier was facing and gazing down at the river when first erected, deliberately so, as Severn lads they would have swam and fished there, a poignant gesture to lost youth. It was re-sited by the river much later, but in the opposite direction, facing the square. If you have time to linger before catching your bus back, turn right after crossing the bridge and walk along the riverside path to find the **old coracle shed** with information about these ancient type of boats and their makers. The last coracle maker, Eustace Rogers, died in 2003. Sailing them continues with August bank holiday coracle regattas, anyone can enter, if you dare to! See www.coracleshed.org for more.

Walking through a World Heritage Site: Ironbridge to Little Wenlock

The **Tontine Hotel** was built in 1780 by the shareholders of the bridge, they hoped the first iron bridge would attract some tourists (it has!) A tontine is an old type of shareholding contract where the last shareholder alive got the whole income. It is allegedly haunted by the last man hanged in Shropshire and other ghosts. Along the river front and at the **Wharfage**, where you cross the road and start your climb out of the Gorge, you can see remains of **old lime kilns** to the right, and to the left the old steps to landing places and the **Coalbrookdale Company Warehouses**. This all

dates back to the time when Ironbridge was an important port, shipping the produce of Gorge industries to other river ports like Gloucester and Bristol. The main landing point at the **Wharfage** has iron rails to help shift cargoes to and from the warehouse. This is now the site of the **Ironbridge Gorge Museum of the River** with free displays and an information centre. On the other side of the car park is the bus station and toilets.

Go down the Wharfage steps to examine the old por

The Rotunda, at the top of **Lincoln Hill** above the Ironbridge Gorge, was built in the early 1790s by the ironmaster Richard Reynolds. It is believed to have been a circular structure with 9 cast-iron pillars and a lead-covered roof. Inside was a revolving sea allowing spectacular panoramic views of the Ironbridge Gorge and The Wrekin. Now only the original brick foundation remains but the views are still outstanding an there is a detailed information board here.

The Iron Bridge is just visible in the light of a November dawn from the Rotunda viewpoint

The sheer drops off the top of **Lincoln Hill** recall that this was once a vast limestone quarry, heavily mined on both sides in the 18th Century for the Coalbrookdale furnaces. You walk along the ridge above the old quarry sides on one of the **Sabbath Walks** with constructed viewpoints from which to admire the Ironbridge Gorge. These **Sabbath Walks** with their follies and attractions (now all sadly disappeared) were first made as a special place for the workers to enjoy on Sundays, hopefully after Church. The bosses thought this was a much better alternative to their workforce spending their one day off at the pub! The paths here are all that are left of one of the first free, laid out public parks in the UK, an idea far ahead of its time. **Severn Gorge Countryside Trust** manages these woods and paths today. Leaflets about these old walks, the modern sculpture seats, the history and geology of the Ironbridge Gorge are all available from their website.

Sabbath Walks viewpoints

As you exit the woodlands, you walk past **Holy Trinity Church**. It was built by the Darby family after they converted from Quakers to the Church of England (so Abraham Darby IV could become a magistrate). You can spot the **Darby tomb** in the churchyard and even some iron headstones. Over the porch is a memorial to a former churchwarden, Captain Webb of Dawley, the first person to swim the English Channel, he died trying to swim over Niagara Falls (some thought it suicidal so his memorial is placed outside the church). The graveyard gives a spectacular viewpoint across Coalbrookdale, including the site of the old **Aga Stove and Range Works**; when they closed in 2017 three hundred years of heavy industry in the Ironbridge Gorge ended.

At the end of Church Road the impressive **Victorian Wesleyan Methodist Chapel** is on your right. As in other mining areas, many workers were non conformists; Baptists, Plymouth Brethren, Quakers and Methodists all had their followers in the local towns and villages. You pass **The Museum of Iron**, the historic buildings are the remains of the great **Coalbrookdale Works** founded by the Darby family. The impressive ruins of the early blast furnace are exhibited in a building (free to enter) behind the pleasant outdoor **Sculpture Garden** picnic spot.

The huge **Coalbrookdale Great Western Railway Viaduct** is a highlight of the Trail, trains crossed here until 2017 when the decommissioning of the Ironbridge power station got underway. **Upper Furnace Pool** was in existence before Abraham Darby came to the Gorge in 1709. It was one of several pools used to store water for

Coalbrookdale's industries and blast furnaces. For excellent information about all these places, including the major buildings and heritage features visible hereabouts, there is a comprehensive leaflet with drawings and explanations available from the **Ironbridge Gorge Museum of Iron**. You can pick up a free copy in the museum shop or download it from their website. To enter the main museum you will need to buy the 'Ironbridge Gorge Museum Passport'.

Look for the information board at the entrance to **Loamhole Dingle**, 'loam' is soil composed of sand, silt and clay. Further up the valley in **Lydebrook Dingle** sandstone was quarried since the C18th, during the Industrial Revolution and after, for the Coalbrookdale ironworks for sand castings to make iron moulds. Today, the silt is collected in a silt trap situated at the beginning of the woodland entrance.

When you leave the dingle you walk for a short way on **The Ropewalk** track which was developed in the early 1700s for horses to pull small tubs of sandstone from Lydebrook Dingle to Coalbrookdale. In the 1750s, a railway was built along this route to connect Horsehay with the Coalbrookdale Works. The long straight track was good for spinning rope too.

On the outskirts of **Little Wenlock** village on your right you pass **St Lawrence's Church**. There has been a church on this site for over 800 years, the village is older and was recorded in The Domesday Book as Wenloch. A leaflet about the history of the church is available.

St Lawrence's Church

Following an Ancient Routeway : Little Wenlock to Wellington

You start your walk around the village following part of the **Little Wenlock Bench Walk** with its many memorial benches sited at excellent viewpoints. All walkers on the Telford T50 Trail should pause and reflect at the **Memorial Bench for David Hutchison**, after whom the **Hutchison Way** from Wellington to Newport is named (see the section, 'optional spur to Newport'). He was the Chief Executive of Wrekin District Council shortly after the new town came into being and a keen walker. He lived in Little Wenlock and died at a relatively young age. David had the vision of preserving Telford's open green spaces and letting the industrial mounds regenerate for us all to enjoy. Without his determination our Trail would not have been possible. Honour David Hutchison's legacy by continuing to campaign to preserve our open green spaces and keep them accessible for all.

Halfway House (formerly *The Wrekin Cottage*) on the path up the Wrekin has had an interesting history as Victorian Tea Rooms and as mini C19th and C20th pleasure grounds, with swing boats, donkey rides and gardens.

Old postcards of Halfway House from Bob Coalbran's collection: www.halfwayhouseonthewrekin.com

Wrekin Cottage, Wellington.

The Wrekin Cottage, Wellington.

There used to be pre-booked bacon sandwiches available when the cafe was open; keen fast walkers ordered them on the way up and ate them on the way down. There are plans to reopen the original tea rooms and restore this place to some of its former glory in the near future. The lack of mains water is the main stumbling block as the old wells and springs that served the buildings are not up to modern demands;however, the new owners are hopeful of overcoming this obstacle. There is an open air kiosk, a pavilion room and a garden with a lovely view of The Ercall to enjoy over a cup of tea and an ice cream. It's been the chosen rest point for well over a hundred years, you will see why!

The Wrekin is a place of ancient history and legend. The track up the Wrekin is one of the oldest 'roads' in Britain, used since the Bronze Age and possibly even before then, as part of a longer route across the country from east to west. It followed the safer high ground above dense lowland forests with their wild animals and places for ambush. Quality flint in the Stone Age, then bronze made from copper and tin and later iron, were traded along these very ancient routes.

There are Bronze Age remains here, including a barrow which is difficult to spot, but you can't fail to see the outlines of a large 20 acre *Iron Age hill fort* with circular ditches and ramparts carved from the rock and soil with hand tools. It was built by the Celtic Cornovii tribe about 2,000 years ago. One can only wonder at the manpower, social organisation and resources needed to construct it and why it was built. This is a brilliant defensive position because you could see the surrounding countryside for miles around in all directions (you still can), and the steep sides would have guaranteed the exhaustion of any attackers (as they now guarantee the exhaustion of many aspirant walkers and mountain bikers). In Iron Age hill forts there are remains of round huts, but not the repeated destruction layers one might expect if this had been an era of warring tribes. Whether they were mainly ceremonial places, large permanent settlements or places of refuge, they show that people had the time and power to accumulate the food and other resources necessary to build huge earth structures. Whatever the reasons for constructing them the results are very impressive. Shropshire has a high density of Iron Age forts; this is one of many very good examples that survive in the County. As you approach the summit there is an information board to your right with pictures to show what the fort might have looked like in prehistoric times. You can still see the signs of the ancient fort's outer and inner gateways now called *'heaven's gate'* and *'hell's gate'* which cleaved through the ramparts and ditches.

South of the summit is a rocky outcrop known as *The Raven's Bowl* and below it are *The Calendar Stones*. This is said to be Shropshire's Stonehenge by local historian George Evans. At noon at each Spring equinox, a shaft of light is said to come through the westerly rock and shine on an easterly rock to make the circular shape of the sun; useful knowledge for an ancient priesthood! The Shropshire Star 21 March 2009 sent a reporter to test out this theory , at the appointed time (10 minutes past 12 local noon) the disc duly appeared.

Calendar stones painting
© George Evans

The Wrekin summit toposcope tells you what all those distant hills and places on the 360 degree horizon are: you can see most of Shropshire and way beyond from here, 17 counties in all. The Wrekin's 407m 1,335 ft summit is a landmark that can be seen from all over too, so don't forget to toast *"all friends around The Wrekin"*. This has always been a useful place for sending messages, from lighting beacons to warn of invasions or to celebrate national events, to erecting C20th radio and TV masts. The white triangular pillar **trig point** is no longer essential for surveying heights and distances in a satellite age. The TV transmitter mast is still there with its red light on the top plus satellite dishes for mobile phones.

If you have children with you, tell them the tale of **The Wrekin Giant** and how he nearly drowned Shrewsbury in revenge, when he found folk from there had stolen his fish from the Severn. He picked up a huge shovel full of earth and was marching to the town to throw it on the inhabitants when a cobbler persuaded him it was so far away it wasn't worth his trouble to walk to Shrewsbury, so he dumped the soil to make The Wrekin instead. A little bit fell off his shovel to form Little Hill and where he scraped the soil from his boots is now The Ercall.

The main east to west route across Britain still skirts The Wrekin but now it follows the bottom of the hill where you enter **Wellington** and go under the **M54 motorway** and then cross over **Holyhead Road**, this is the old **Roman Road** known as **Watling Street**. It was rebuilt by Thomas Telford as the main coaching route between London, Wales and Ireland, then it became the A5 in the motor age and was degraded to a B road when the motorway was built alongside it.

Your way treads a prehistoric path that cleaves through the ramparts of an Iron Age Hill fort, still clearly visible. The Wrekin's extensive viewpoint has been used as a signal post past and present. The beacon was lit for the Millennium celebrations 31 December 1999. It is a popular gathering place to see in the New Year and by tradition, a place to greet friends on New Year's Day.

Shropshire's Ancient Market Town : Wellington

Wellington has claims to be the oldest market town in Shropshire, its proximity to the Roman Road would have certainly attracted traders. Its Saxon name *Weo-leah-ingaton*, meaning the 'settlement by the temple in the grove' shows it predates the Christian Mercians who ruled here in the sixth century AD. It is recorded in the Domesday Book.

In Norman times houses were clustered around a market green in front of the church. In 1244 a market charter was granted by King Henry III and the market was moved to the current **Market Square**. The present indoor market was built in 1856 when a group of businessmen bought the 1244 market rights from the Lords of the Manor (the Forester family).

The Trail goes down a narrow enclosed medieval road called Ten Tree Croft. The name derives from Tenter Croft, a smallholding with a field where cloth was stretched on wooden frames and held in place with tenter hooks.

You can still see the original narrow medieval streets, alleys and market squares in the present day layout of the town with buildings surviving from medieval, Georgian and Victorian times to today, many are listed for their architectural or historic value. Walkers interested in history can download a copy of the **Made in Wellington Mural Trail** and look out for the pictures of past trades and famous people as you pass by, it starts in Larkin Way (a clue to one of them is in the name). A fascinating history of the town, its buildings and people is available on line from Wellington Town Council website www.wellington-shropshire.gov.uk

Civil War Battles and Early Industry on Stage 4 of the Trail

There have been castles in **Apley Woods** since 1270. **Apley Castle** was the site of two Civil War battles when different branches of the Charlton family fought on opposing sides to control it. It changed hands between Royalist and Parliament forces twice. The next Charlton generation was involved in plots to put the Duke of Monmouth on the throne and also in the 'glorious revolution' to replace James with William and Mary. You can read about family splits, what happened in the Civil War and in later Stuart times to the Charltons, and the original castle on the *Apley Woods website.* Wellington's coat of arms, pictured right, shows the 'Charlton family lion', Apley Castle, its portcullis and two fleur de lys represent its recapture by the Royalist forces.

The Charlton family started to build a new 'castle' in 1791 but all that remains today are the extensive landscaped gardens and grounds which you walk through on the trail, and an C18th dovecote and ice house which still stand complete on the site. In 1955 the family had to pay two sets of death duties, the estate and Georgian mansion became too expensive to maintain and so it was sold and demolished. **Apley Woods** are now owned and managed by Telford & Wrekin Council. Little remains of the first castle: what was left of the medieval Great Hall, C14th chapel and castle ruins were converted into modern housing. Surrounding farm buildings and some C18th and C19th stables, were built reusing some of the castle masonry. These buildings retain some of the remaining original features. There is a history and tree trail walk you can follow around the estate to see what survives, downloadable from the *Apley Woods website.* The website also has detailed information which continues the story of the Charlton descendents into modern times and pictures of Apley, past and present.

All that's left of the 1791 mansion house 'castle' are its extensive gardens

A few ruins of the original castle are incorporated into more modern buildings.

Today **Steeraway** is a farm but there is an industrial past hereabouts. A tramway linking Steeraway to Watling Street was known to exist in the late 1730s when limestone extraction was stimulated by local iron making. In the 1800s there was at least one deep shaft as we know a 45ft seam was being worked in 1842; however, fluxing limestone was probably exhausted by the mid C19. In 1882 when mining resumed at Steeraway, there were several shafts, levels and kilns. In 1900 mining ceased, and the kilns closed c 1918 . There was a major strike and riot here involving miners (and minors) in 1831.

Limekiln Wood has a long history of C18th and C19th mining and quarrying. The only obvious feature that you can see today is a deep hollow to the left of the trail where you can look down into the top of a ruined lime kiln (take care if tempted to peer in, it's unfenced, see picture below). The limestone was heated to a high temperature using charcoal originally, and later coal, to produce quicklime for mortar, lime for improving soil fertility and later a flux for smelting iron in Coalbrookdale's furnaces.

There is a large former mining area between **Short Wood** and **New Works.** Coal seams are very near the surface here and mining continued until the present century. The former open cast pits have only recently been restored to green fields, though the old pit mounds and deeper shafts that surround the open cast site have long reverted to woodland, with scrub and a few pools in the wetter areas. There are many information boards about coal mining and the restoration of the site as you pass through. Between **New Works** and **Lawley** the route uses **the trundle**, this was originally conceived as an all ability route from Lawley to The Wrekin, but only the section from Lawley to New Works was actually built.

You can spot the remains of limekilns in many places on the Telford T50 50 Mile Trail

An Age of Heavy Industry 1750s to 1950s: Horsehay to Priorslee

Spring Village, Horsehay is a conservation area with an industrial past. It includes the philanthropic *Old Row and New Row* cottages built by the Darby family in the 1750s and 1830s respectively. These were dwellings for the 'principal workmen' in the Coalbrookdale Company Works iron furnaces and foundries. *Horsehay Pool* was the old furnace pool.

In 1857 *Horsehay and Dawley Station* was opened and leased for passenger service by the Great Western Railway in 1861. The site of the station is now home to the *Telford Steam Railway*, a charity set up in the early 1970's to restore steam locomotives for display in the Victorian train sheds. At various times in the year the rail engines are steamed up and run on the restored part of the line. The very popular Polar

Express runs at Xmas. The Trust's ambition is to get steam trains running again from here across the Coalbrookdale Viaduct and into the Ironbridge power station site as a major tourist attraction, but there are real problems with raising the funding to do this. *Lawley Common* is fast disappearing under a huge new housing development. As you walk along it look out for a sign to your right and divert a few yards to spot the remains of *Lawley Village Station and Sidings*, restored by the Telford Steam Trust in 2015.

After *Lawley* the trail visits a Grade II listed tramway bridge in *Newdale*, pictured right. It then joins an old railway line (opened in 1857) which ran from *Lightmoor* to *Ketley*. You will see evidence of old tramways and railways on the rest of your walk; on some tracks eroded grooves for the lines and paving are still visible.

The **Ketley** area is rich in history. The route passes along **Red Lees** (a former tramway) for a short distance and turns off before the **Ketley inclined plane** and **Ketley Hall**. This Grade II listed building was the home of Joseph Reynolds, son of Richard Reynolds and father of William Reynolds. Around 1818 it was occupied by Henry Williams, the engineer and superintendent of the Shropshire Canal Company. The **Ketley Canal**, completed in 1788, brought coal and ironstone to Ketley ironworks from Oakengates, where it later joined the **Shropshire Canal**. The canal included the first successful canal inclined plane in Britain, devised by William Reynolds and situated immediately southwest of his home at Ketley Hall. The canal also took coal and iron via the Shropshire Canal to Horsehay and Coalbrookdale and brought in limestone from

Lincoln Hill (in Madeley) and Buildwas. The incline was disused by 1818. East of the incline lay a coal wharf, which the canal apparently still served from Oakengates in 1842. By the 1880s, however, that surviving length had been abandoned. Our trail passes the remains of the canal, pictured right.

Ketley canal: Ketley Paddock Mound

Your route follows part of the line of the **Roman Road Watling St** towards the old town of **Oakengates.** The town's name derives from the ancient British Celtic *Usc* meaning water and the Norse Viking word *Gate* meaning a road. A large metal sign at the bottom of the main street explains the origin of its name and the history of the town. Like many other places in Telford this

This underpass is on an old dead straight Roman road!

BEVELEY ROAD
SUBWAY
CONSTRUCTED IN 1977
ON THE LINE OF
THE ROMAN ROAD
WATLING STREET

area around **Oakengates** was a centre for coal mining and iron working and it remained important for manufacturing well into the C20th. The most important employer in the area was the **Lilleshall Company**, a huge heavy engineering company founded in 1802 that made winding, pumping and blast engines and during the C19th it made railway locomotives too. Its operations also included coal mining, iron and steel making and brick works and it even had its own railway network. During the 1960s it still employed 750 people making rolled steel products, glazed bricks and sanitary ware. Unfortunately, like much of British manufacturing it declined and by the 1980s its last offices in **Priorslee** were finally closed, though the company still makes plastic components in a remaining factory in Newbury. You will walk past many former pit mounds, balance and furnace pools, old rail and tramways and many buildings and places associated with it on stages 6 and 7 around **The Nabb, Wrockwardine Wood, Cockshutt, Granville Country Park** and **Priorslee.**

This photo shows pools made from flash water from local collieries (now Priorslee Lake, known locally as The Flash). You can also see the Lilleshall Company Mineral Line to Woodhouse Colliery, Woodhouse Lane and Farm. There are many interesting photos and stories about The Lilleshall Co., its buildings and its workers, all available from www.theminerswalk.org.

There is a walking trail you can follow to learn more about the **Lilleshall Company**'s workers, its operations and former buildings in **St Georges** and **Priorslee** called *The Miners Walk* which has a website with extensive information. A leaflet called *The Cockshutt Walk around countryside and heritage on your doorstep* pinpoints the important industrial heritage features that predate the Lilleshall Company including **John Wilkinson's world's first working blast furnaces**.

The main track on the east side of **The Cockshutt** is known locally as **'the pig rails'**. This is the route of an early horse drawn iron rail tramway which carried coal and ironstone from local mines to the furnaces at Donnington Wood. There are the remains of an engine house and an inclined plane. (There are rival claims by Broseley, where John Wilkinson lived and also built blast furnaces, as to which place built the world's first working blast furnaces and iron rail tramways!)

The T50 follows many old tramways and rail lines used to transport raw minerals and pig iron in Stages 5,6,&7, in places their grooves and tracks are still visible.

The Granvilles and their Monuments: Lilleshall to Priorslee

On 8 Sept 1764 Earl Granville Leveson Gower formed a partnership with the Gilbert brothers to develop the mineral resources on his lordship's east Shropshire estates. This was the start of the enterprise that became the **Lilleshall Company** in 1802. Information about them and the foundation of the original company, can be found on the *Friends of Granville Country Park* website. In **Granville Country Park** you can see the old C18th c**anal basin** and the impressive ruins of the **Old Lodge Furnaces** (three immense C19th blast furnaces), each with very detailed information boards. Close to **Granville Country Park** are the sites of two large coal mines, **The Granville Pit** started in 1860 and the **Grange Colliery** which began in 1864, both were nationalised in 1947. In 1951 the two mines were connected underground and from 1952 the Grange served mainly to ventilate the Granville. In 1979 the Granville colliery, which employed 560 men, was closed. It was the last deep coal mine in Shropshire. *The Granville Heritage Trail* is a free leaflet available about the history you can explore here.

C19th blast furnaces in Granville Country Park

Remains of the C18th canal basin

There is one further link between Granville Leveson Gower and our trail and that is the **Lilleshall Sutherland Monument.** There is also an unexpected connection between Lilleshall and the notorious highland clearances. Earl Gower's eldest son George Granville Leveson Gower inherited fabulous wealth from family members involved in the early iron and coal industries. He then made more money through the Lilleshall Company and his own involvement in those industries. Through his marriage to the Countess of Sutherland he also controlled the wealth from vast Scottish estates. He became an influential politician and eventually was granted a dukedom, becoming the first Duke of Sutherland. When he died he was reputed to be the richest man in the UK, possibly the richest in the world. Some of his fortune was used to fund the cost of expelling his Scottish tenants from their land to turn it over to sheep grazing.

The Duke used some of his wealth to improve the road networks, bridges, farming methods and drainage locally which is why his Shropshire farmer tenants were grateful enough to all pitch in and fund the cost of the **Lilleshall Sutherland Monument** to his memory (one wonders whether any would wish to risk declining but perhaps that is just modern cynicism). The "Dukes Drive", Kynnersley Drive, is the lane that leads directly from Kynnersley to the Duke's memorial at Lilleshall. The descendants of his Scottish tenants, who were reduced to destitution, curse his memory to this day (his statue in Scotland has been repeatedly vandalised and there is a modern memorial to the victims of the clearances). His direct descendent, the fifth Duke of Sutherland, sold off the family estates in England at the outbreak of WW1, the last of which to go was the main family home at **Lilleshall Hall**, and in 1917 he moved to London. The imposing Sutherland stately home is now **Lilleshall National Sports and Conferencing Centre**.

At Lilleshall, views of and from the Monument are a trail highlight.

> **The inscription on the Lilleshall Sutherland Monument reads:-**
>
> *"To the memory of George Granville Leveson Gower KG. First Duke of Sutherland. The most just and generous of landlords. This monument is erected by the occupiers of his Grace's Shropshire farms as a public testimony that he went down to his grave with the blessings of his tenants on his head and left behind him upon his estates the best inheritance which a gentleman of England can bequeath to his son men ready to stand by his house heart and hand. 1833".*

Readers may be interested to know that the Scottish estates still remain but in a different branch of the family. The Duke had no direct male heirs and women cannot inherit titles under English law. However, Scottish law is different and women can inherit titles so what remains of the Sutherland estates in Scotland, together with most of the family fortune derived from the industrial revolution described in this guide, have passed not to the present Duke, a third cousin, but down the female line through a niece, the Countess of Sutherland and to her descendants.

Lilleshall was a village in Saxon times, it is recorded in the Domesday Book. There is an interesting Norman Church which has another connection with the Granvilles; it was extensively restored in Victorian times by the Duchess of Sutherland. The ruined medieval **Lilleshall Abbey** is some distance from the trail, so a diversion on foot to see it is best left for another time.

Wildlife on the Telford T50 50 Mile Trail

On the trail you will walk through five Sites of Special Scientific Interest (SSSIs) and fourteen Local Nature Reserves (LNRs) with more LNR designations in the pipeline. This is a walk of outstanding quality and variety for anyone interested in geology, ecology, flora and fauna with some nationally rare examples present. Pocket field guides or equivalent smart phone apps for wildflowers, birds and butterflies will be useful companions if you plan to explore the trail in more detail.

A large amount of the trail takes you through woods. Some areas are remnants of ancient woods but most are secondary woodlands where old industrial areas have been left alone for vegetation to regenerate and animals to colonise. In addition, around 15 million trees were planted by Telford Development Corporation from the late 1960s to cover brownfield sites and land contaminated by heavy industry and to deliberately create a 'forest city'. Many woodlands are owned by Telford & Wrekin Council and managed by not-for-profit enterprises such as the **Small Woods Association** and **Severn Gorge Countryside Trust.**

The **Telford Town Park LNR** is in the south of the Park. It is of major ecological importance. The reserve contains pools, pit mounds, heathland, woodlands, meadows and grasslands which have all been allowed to 'rewild' on former brownfield sites. There are many information boards about the large numbers of insects, amphibians, birds, mammals and wildflowers which can be found here. Even adders have been spotted. With amphibians being particularly under pressure in the UK, the large number of pools and wetlands in the park form an important refuge for them, including a population of great crested newts. The only species of amphibian not recorded here is the palmate newt, so if you spot one do tell!

You can follow a self guided *Telford Town Park Nature Trail* to explore the LNR. Free leaflets are available from the Town Park Information Centre to the right of the start of the Telford T50 50 Mile Trail or from their web site, or follow the links on the Telford T50 50 Mile Trail website.

Telford Town Park Nature Trail with its many pools

Most common (and some rare) woodland, water and meadowland species of flora can be seen here. Butterflies and dragonflies are colourful and abundant in summer and over sixty species of woodland, meadowland and water birds are present, together with some seasonal migrating visitors. There are no hides but if you move quietly through the area with a pair of binoculars you will usually notice something of interest, and if you see what looks like a partly plucked pigeon at your feet, you may have just disturbed a recent sparrowhawk kill.

A peacock butterfly has 'eyespots' to confuse predators

The mixed habitat area around **Madeley Court Woods and Pools** has a self guided nature trail described in *Nature Walks in Madeley Parish* available from Madeley Town Council. The publication *Nature Walks in Brookside and Stirchley Parish* also has a nature trail you can follow called *Madebrook Pools and Telford Town Park.* All can be downloaded as pdfs from the Telford & Wrekin Council website.

Dawley Hamlets LNR,with its pools and wooded pit mounds, is another area that has regenerated naturally. The pools are popular with bats (some roost in old tunnels and mine shafts). Weighing less than a 20p piece, match box sized common pipistrelle bats hunt by zig zagging 2 to 10m above the pools, eating up to 3,000 gnats a night. Daubenton's bats use their feet to fish insects from the surface water. Wet habitat species here include great crested newts and an aquatic plant called Marestail.

The restocked Dawley Pools are popular with anglers (and bats!): photo Maria Bagnall

The **Rough Park** area was once mined for coal and clay to supply local industries. It is now a LNR of woods and open meadows managed by Telford and Wrekin Council. Look behind you at the picnic tables and you can see the remains of big spoil heaps. The area hereabouts is worth exploring in the late spring and early summer for wild orchids and meadowland wild flowers which attract many species of butterflies. The woods are attractive for woodland birds (look and listen for woodpeckers and jays), butterflies and bats. There is a self guided Rough Park nature trail with details of interesting and rare species recorded here in *Nature Walks in Madeley Parish* (see our website for pdf download links).

red kite:© Tim Preston

jay: © Tim Preston

The trail then takes you through **Lodge Field and Beeches Field Local Nature Reserves**, these two small reserves help to create a green corridor for wildlife and for walkers, between **Rough Park** and **Lloyds Coppice** and the extensive woodlands on both sides of the Ironbridge Gorge. Both **Lodge Field LNR** and **Beeches Field LNR** are owned by Telford and Wrekin Council and managed by local volunteers. **Lodge Field** used to be a children's play area but it became overgrown with scrub and brambles until an enthusiastic group of local volunteers took on the management and worked hard to get it established as a LNR over 10 years ago. **Beeches Field** was the site of a brick and tile works, then partially let for horse grazing but otherwise neglected until another group of volunteers took on the management, improved the habitats and got it established as a LNR in 2017. There are grasslands rich in flowers supporting butterflies and moths in the summer: 2478 spotted and marsh orchids were counted on the **Lodge Field** in June 2019! In **Beeches Field** there is a pond that is important for dragonflies and great crested newts. **Lodge Field** hosts an annual community picnic and both LNRs organise wildlife events for children. The views from these fields are superb. The ground rises steeply above the river in the Ironbridge Gorge so there are thermal currents much enjoyed by buzzards, kestrels and ravens and occasionally by red kites passing through. You have a good chance of seeing buzzards soaring above you in the Gorge here.

A protected species, great crested newts grow up to 16cm, males have wavy crests in the breeding season

Lloyds Coppice is an ancient semi-natural woodland of 40 hectares steeped in history, although our trail does not explore the many historic remains in the wood. It is one of the woodlands managed by **Severn Gorge Countryside Trust**, (SGCT) which was set up in 1991 to look after 260 hectares of land for the benefit of wildlife, local people and visitors. The Trust is responsible for over half of the land within the **Ironbridge Gorge World Heritage Site**, managing an important SSSI landscape with some endangered species. **Lloyds Coppice** once lay at the southerly end of the Wrekin Forest, an area that was subject to 'forest law' in medieval times and has been managed since at least the 1600s. This woodland grows in sandstone, clay and coal; it supports a wide range of tree species such as sweet chestnut, field maple, small-leaved lime, yews and wild service. There are remnants of ancient woodland flowers such as yellow archangel. However, much of the woodland was felled for fuel during the 1st and 2nd World Wars and so very few veteran trees exist. Of the 574 species of invertebrate recorded within Lloyds Coppice, several are species new to Shropshire, or are nationally scarce. The heathland is cared for and monitored by SGCT volunteers and staff and it

yellow archangel

hosts a large number of species including toads, mice, butterflies, spiders and beetles. Of the 49 species of spider recorded, 40 of them were found only in the heathland reflecting its importance as a habitat. There are several small pools, one of which supports the great crested newt.

If you walk from Ironbridge up to the **Rotunda** at the top of **Lincoln Hill** above the Gorge in late spring you will be rewarded by the stunning display, and smell, of wild garlic and woodland flowers and in the autumn by fungi.

Lincoln Hill is an SSSI for its flora, limestone geology and its fossils. It's an uplifted sea bed, formed 432m years ago when Ironbridge lay south of the Equator. Records show that these woods have been exploited for timber and fuel since at least the C13th, so not many ancient trees remain here, though the woods as you exit onto Church Road have a few veteran beech trees. New species, including false acacia, were introduced by the Reynolds family when the **Sabbath Walks** were created and the woodlands replanted.

wild garlic

The steep sides of the woodlands between the **Rotunda** and Church Road are old limestone quarries. Here you are standing above ancient coral reefs formed around 400 million years ago when this area was just south of the equator. The rocks are the fossilised remains of algae, corals and other sea creatures that lived in the tropical waters. This part of the Earth's crust has since drifted northwards due to a process called plate tectonics (continental drift). There is more information about these woodlands in *The Sabbath Walks Trail* and *Iron Trail* leaflets published by SGCT, all freely available from local information centres. There are excellent walking trails around **Lloyds Coppice** and **Lincoln Hill**, with a detailed written guide in *Nature Walks in The Gorge Parish* (you can follow links and download pdfs via our website).

The large **Upper Furnace Pool** in Coalbrookdale has two streams flowing into it from the north-east and north-west. Today, it's a well-established pool for wildlife, look for great reedmace, dragonflies, warblers and water birds as you pass by.

Loamhole Dingle is a wet, ancient semi-natural woodland with mainly ash, alder, silver birch and hazel. In late Spring you can enjoy the wildflowers before the canopy grows dense and shades out the light. May is a good time to visit as you can spot birds while they collect food for nestlings. The Lyde Brook flows from the north-west, through the dingle into **Upper Furnace Pool** and onward along the water courses of Coalbrookdale towards the River Severn at the bottom of the valley. Take time to explore and move quietly, you may spot woodpeckers, grey wagtails and dippers or even bank voles if you are lucky.

When you exit **Loamhole Dingle**, you walk along the **Ropewalk** track before you enter **Lydebrook Dingle** woods. Look at the meadows on the left of the track. The **Wilderness Meadow** is a species rich unimproved grassland. After the flowers and grasses have set seeds the meadows here are cut for hay and then grazed in the autumn by a flock of Soay sheep (pictured above); this helps maintain the diversity of meadow flowers you see here in spring and summer. These types of meadowland are now rare in the UK, so these fields are of national importance, just short of SSSI status. The rare breed Soays are closely related to their prehistoric domesticated ancestors. The *Loamhole Dingle: History under your feet* (SGCT) walking leaflet has information about the viaduct pools, Loamhole, Lydebrook and Ropewalk area.

Lydebrook Dingle is an SSSI for its flora, fauna and geological importance with unusual tufa deposits from the lime rich water and exposures of the coal measure rocks. Trees along the water's edge create a natural habitat for invertebrates; the aquatic larvae of the rare crane fly, Lipsothrix nigristigma, thrives in the saturated woody debris. Giant horsetails in the wet woodlands are living fossils, the much smaller relatives of the huge 20m horsetail trees which grew here profusely in the Carboniferous period 300 million years ago; their remains helped lay down the coal seams of Coalbrookdale. The wildflower rich **Loamhole** and **Lydebrook Dingle Woods** have beautiful displays of wild garlic in late May. Dog's mercury is common as it is in other former mining areas. Fallow and muntjac deer, badgers and bats live here but you will be lucky to spot them. SGCT is trying to exclude deer from the woods to prevent tree damage.

giant horsetails

Lydebrook Dingle. Rock exposures of geological importance are visible at many points along the trail though some are inaccessible. Please don't hammer or collect.

Wenlocks Wood is a good place to enjoy displays of bluebells in late Spring and between here and the **Wrekin Woods** and you might spot fallow deer, especially if you are walking solo and into the wind, early morning or evening. The oak and ash trees used to be coppiced to provide wood to make charcoal. The hazel trees were coppiced to make baskets, fences, walking sticks, bean poles, in fact anything where straight thin strips of wood would be useful. You can see the evidence of coppicing where a number of tree trunks are growing outwards from a base, some pointing out at strange angles. Trees were cut just above the base leaving a stump called a 'stool'. The wood soon began to re-grow with a multiplicity of new shoots around the stool, which could be harvested again and again a few years later. The hazel here is also home to dormice. The **Wrekin Woods** in Shropshire on the west side,owned by The Raby Estate, have modern conifer soft wood plantations, in contrast to the native woods on the east side in Telford which we walk through.

The geology of **The Wrekin** and **The Ercall** covers an immense period of time from the Precambrian Era, the Wrekin's oldest rocks are 677m years old, to the post-glacial sands, clays and gravels of the last 10,000 years. **The Wrekin** and **The Ercall** are 'volcanic' in origin but these hills are not the remains of ancient volcanoes. Some rocks found on **The Wrekin** were formed by ancient lava and ash flows spewed out from volcanic islands in ancient seas, when there were only soft bodied creatures inhabiting the oceans. **The Ercall** has other types of volcanic rocks where the hot molten magma pushed its way into other rocks from underground but did not reach the surface. One rock here called granophyre is similar to the granite rocks of Cornwall, however, the molten rock cooled faster as it reached much nearer the surface, therefore the quartz and other crystals which formed are much smaller than the ones found in granite, which formed at greater depths. These very hard volcanic rocks have resisted millions of years of erosion so they are left above the surface as hills, while the many younger softer sedimentary rocks that covered them later have been worn away. This is why **The Wrekin** and **The Ercall** stand out in such a dramatic way in the landscape today.

The Ercall Quarry is a geological site of international importance, look for the dividing line between the pink and grey rocks!

The Ercall also shows us the dividing point in time where life on earth exploded in its complexity, when hard bodied creatures just started to evolve. This transition point between the Pre-Cambrian and Cambrian, seen here as the dividing line between the pink volcanic rocks and the grey sandstones, is internationally recognised by geologists for its importance in earth history. The **Ercall Quarry** and the famous **'Ercall unconformity'** helped C19th and C20th scientists piece together our understanding of the Earth's history and evolution. Darwin studied these rocks and their fossils (spot the carving of a trilobite as you enter The Ercall Woods).

There is even a fossilised beach, with remains of ripples in the mud and creatures from ancient Cambrian seas. Later deposits include limestones, coal, sand and gravels. From prehistoric times to about 40 years ago the area has been mined and quarried for its metals and building materials. **The Ercall** is studied by geologists from all over the world. An information display board is at the foot of the quarry to your left. The variety

Fossil ripple beds

in the type of rocks means there is a corresponding diversity in the trees and flowers that grow here and the creatures that feed on them. **The Wrekin Forest** and **The Ercall** are SSSIs. There are a number of native trees present including oak, ash, birch, holly, hazel, willow and there are impressive beech woods (unusual in Shropshire) on the sandier quartzite soils, as you descend through **Wrekin Woods.** There are huge veteran trees here that have survived previous logging and coppicing.

The **Ercall Woods** are similarly rich in tree species with a few old survivors. There are ancient yew trees in both woods which is unusual. Some wonder if this might be because our forebears thought it unlucky to cut down a yew tree; echoes of a long distant past perhaps? There are many speculations about the origins of the old superstitions concerning yews, and their association with churchyards. However, the very dense nature of these extremely long living evergreens make them good nesting habitats for small woodland birds.

Pied flycatchers come from West Africa to breed: © G. Bishton

On the thin sandy soils on both summits are heather, wavy-hair grass, and bilberries. In the woods there are bluebells, wood anemone, wood sorrel, wild garlic, honeysuckle, bryony, nightshade and an enormous species count of fungi, butterflies, moths and other insects including solitary and bumble bees. Nest boxes encourage woodland birds to breed and pied flycatchers have recently started returning to these woods. There are herds of roe, fallow and muntjac deer.

The Ercall is also important nationally and internationally for fungi and invertebrates; 821 species of invertebrates were found here in just one single survey. It is managed by **Shropshire Wildlife Trust** and there is an information board about its ecology on your right as you leave the road and enter **The Ercall Woods. The Ercall quarry i**s home to the dingy skipper, a rare type of butterfly, that lives on the warm rocks and feeds on a yellow-flowered plant called birdsfoot trefoil. The author has spotted peregrines, kestrels, buzzards and sparrowhawk around the woods and quarries here.

The Wrekin SSSI has remnants of ancient woodlands with some veteran trees.

Dothill LNR is owned by Telford & Wrekin Council and maintained by local volunteers. It is a quiet oasis for wildlife in the middle of a residential area, surrounded by main roads, and comprises three main areas: **Dothill Pool, Tee Lake** and **Beanhill Valley**. The largest lake, **Tee Lake,** was created by the Forester family during the C17th as part of formal gardens around their house, *Dothill Park.* The hillock on the east side was created from the excavated material from the lake. It was one of the grandest houses of its time, but the family moved to *Willey Park* in 1740 and it fell into disuse in the C19th. The ruin was demolished in 1960. There are lakes, streams, woods, marshes and open meadow habitats resulting in a diverse ecology with a large number of species recorded for such a small area. Eighty two species of birds have been recorded at **Dothill LNR**, including kingfishers and rare breeding lesser spotted woodpeckers; it is one of those places where anything can turn up, and often does, from goosanders to flocks of goldcrest, to a peregrine and a red kite. There is a downloadable leaflet and map available about the reserve and the **50 Tree Trail** (this too was a project to celebrate Telford's 50th anniversary.)Kingfishers breed at many other pools along the trail and along the Severn; look out for a fast disappearing flash of iridescent blue, flying low over water.

© Tim Preston

Six species of bats have been seen flying over **Tee Lake** inlcuding common and soprano pipistrelles, noctule and Daubenton's. A large number of butterfly species have been recorded feeding on the wide variety wildflowers. Even an otter has been spotted! To see Tim Preston's photos of the flowers, birds and butterflies seen here, visit the Dothill Local Nature Reserve Facebook Page.

With its 56 acres of meadows, pools, trees and winding footpaths, **Apley Woods** is a very fine example of C19th landscape woodland. Records mention woodland on the site as far back as 1300. However, the present woods were largely created during the last 200 years as part of the ornamental gardens to the Georgian Apley Castle mansion, since demolished.

Rare lesser spotted woodpeckers breed at Dothill. © Tim Preston

The open water and reedbeds of Aoley pool and its adjacent scrubland sustain a rich diversity of wildlife. Many species can be found in this important nature reserve. As the site has many bank voles, wood mice and other rodents it is good for both tawny and barn owls. There are moths, butterflies, dragonflies and damselflies and six species of bats with bat boxes in the woods to help them. Apley has a fine collection of trees which range from semi-natural woodland to ornamental specimens from all over the world. Of particular note is the **Yew Avenue**, thought to be 300 years old, and the large red oak which is mentioned in Andrew Morton's book, *"Trees of Shropshire"*, as one of the outstanding specimens in the county. Look for the amazing examples of woodland art, sculptures of birds of prey and woodland animals. Some may be higher than you think!

Limekiln Wood LNR was once part of the Royal Forest of Wrekin, and as one might guess the underlying rocks are limestone. The woods are full of limestone loving flora, including the wood's speciality, wild orchids; if the leaves have spots, it's a common spotted orchid, marsh orchids are also found on old industrial sites. The wood is of great botanical interest with 150 recorded plant species .

Bats roost in the old adits and mine shafts that occur in **Limekiln Wood** and the nearby **Steeraway**. A large herd of fallow deer roams across the whole area, including in the neighbouring **Short Wood** and the former mining district around **New Works**. Your best chance to spot them would be to walk alone, early morning, late afternoon or in the evening when there are fewer people and dogs around. There is a useful leaflet produced by *Shropshire Wildlife Trust*, about the woodlands between The Wrekin and New Works, if you want to find out more.

Smalley Hill Nature Reserve, which you pass on your right, is an old landfill site. It has more habitat variety than one might expect, with areas of rough grasslands supporting soft rush and tufted hair grass and mosses, ponds where great crested newts and dragonflies live, plus a number of hedgerows. It is a butterfly heaven. Kestrels can often be seen hovering, hunting for field voles and wood mice. The management of **Smalley Hill** by *Shropshire Wildlife Trust* has been made possible thanks to the support of Veolia, who also sponsored the Telford T50 50 Mile Trail.

Ketley Paddock Mound site is a small LNR, an 11 acre public open space owned by Telford & Wrekin Council. From the main mound which rises to 500 feet, you can see magnificent views to the West and North. The **Paddock Mound** site comprises two mounds with adjacent pasture and three water bodies, the largest of which is the remnant of the **Ketley Canal**. The site was formed by coal and iron ore working in the 18th century but nature has now reclaimed the abandoned pit mounds and canal. The mound to the south is the more accessible and well walked. The **"Plantation"** mound to the north is heavily wooded and less accessible. The vegetation is mostly mixed woodland of oak and birch, and acidic grassland. There

is a good range of woodland and water birds, both resident and visiting, plus the more common species of mammals, amphibians and butterflies that use the reserve. However, the site will soon be completely surrounded by urban development and this will add enormously to its importance as a sanctuary for wildlife and a quiet retreat for local people. There is a large information board if you want to find out more.

Ketley Millennium Village has an interesting mix of styles and tenure and is well landscaped. It is surrounded by *Land Trust open space* which is managed as a nature reserve with several waymarked routes.

Ketley Paddock Mound bus stop with wildlife art work

You walk through a patchwork of small woods and green open spaces on the final stages of the trail. Some of these habitats are being improved by a team of community volunteers from **St Georges** for birds, wildflowers and insects. A 2018 count on the tree lined, heathland south facing slopes of **Albion Bank**, found 13 butterfly species. **The Cockshutt** is a good place on the trail for spotting birds including whitethroats, jays, linnets, willow warblers, green woodpeckers, and chiffchaffs. There are pipistrelle bats and many butterflies including green hairstreaks and the dingy skipper. The woods, replanted by **The Lilleshall Company**, are now a local wildlife site containing regenerating wet areas, scrub and grassy banks. It is being proposed as a LNR. There is a leaflet available about its history, nature trails and the species recorded here; to download it and find out more, follow a link on our website.

At **Muxton Marsh** impeded drainage caused by spoil dumping has formed a wetland. This tiny oasis is an SSSI, a nationally rare example of unimproved low lying grassland and marshy fen vegetation with a range of fescue grasses, sedges and rushes, including marsh fox-tail, sweet vernal-grass, carnation sedge, toad rush and jointed rush, greater reed mace, yellow flag water iris and water horsetails. Common spotted orchid, meadow vetchling, bird's-foot trefoil, eyebright and yellow rattle are among the large number of meadow species that flourish in the rough grasssland cut for hay here. At the foot of the slope of the pit-mound there is a zone of wet loving trees, dominated by grey willow with small amounts of alder and crack willow. There are bog mosses, including sphagnum which forms a carpet beneath the willows. The dryer slope above is occupied by oak and silver birch with a few characteristic woodland plants, including wood anemone, yellow archangel and dog's mercury.

dingy skipper
butterfly-conservation.org

Not surprisingly the site is popular with butterflies including the rare dingy skipper, moths, bees, dragonflies and other insects. The brook that feeds the marsh and the fen teems with aquatic life including freshwater shrimp, diving beetles, caddis fly larvae, minnows and frogs. Both **Muxton Marsh** and **Granville Country Park** are owned by Telford &Wrekin Council and managed by Shropshire Wildlife Trust.

"Who would call a butterfly dingy? Poor thing. It's actually beautifully marked in mottled browns and buff, which means it's perfectly camouflaged against rocks and bare soil where it likes to bask. We have 8 different skippers in Britain that can be mistaken for moths because of the way they hold their wings. Sadly, like many of our butterflies, dingy skipper numbers have dropped drastically but Telford's post-industrial landscape is a regional stronghold." John Hughes, Shropshire Wildlife Trust.

Lilleshall Hill became Telford's newest LNR in 2019. Trees and gorse cover the lower slopes while the top remains grassy and heath like. The hill rises 132m high with outstanding views as far as the Berwyns and is surrounded by open farmland, this makes it an oasis for birds, butterflies and bats.

Granville Country Park is a large LNR with the remains of an old canal and feeder pools providing wetland habitats for marsh vegetation, dragonflies, damselflies and water birds. There are many acres of new woodlands which have been colonised by a number of bird, insects and woodland flower species. Former coal mines, industrial sites, pit mounds and spoil heaps are now meadows and heaths full of wild flower rich grassland. Orchids, ox-eye daisy, cowslips and yellow rattle and a number of other meadowland plants and grasses have miraculously re-appeared here after nearly becoming extinct in the neighbouring farmlands as a result

Common darter dragonfly: i darts out to surprise its prey!

of modern farming practices. Bird's-foot trefoil is common and feeds the caterpillars of Telford's two speciality, rare but locally thriving, butterflies: the dingy skipper and green hairstreak. From the tops of the mounds one can see for miles around and the whole area is very popular with walkers and riders and merits more exploration. Look out for the beautiful wood sculptures of some of the wildlife you might spot here.

Priorslee Lake (The Flash) is home to a number of bat species. A very rare native bat that only weighs between 6 and 15g and can fit inside a match box, Nathusius' pipistrelle, has been recorded here. These tiny animals are tougher than you might guess, they have been recorded migrating between Britain and Latvia and Lithuania. This is a popular birding spot in Shropshire and there is a *Friends of Priorslee* website that records sightings, so you can check before you visit what birds to look out for.

The last LNR on our trail is *Randlay Valley*, which includes *Randlay Woods.* These grasslands, streams and pools form an important corridor linking the Town Park LNR with other green corridors to the east and west. The sunken circular picnic area by *Randlay Pool*, as you re-enter the Town Park, is a lovely spot in summer to sit and watch the butterflies feeding on the wildflower edges. This is a perfect place to rest at the end of your Telford T50 50 Mile Trail walk and reflect on your experiences of exploring Telford's newest long distance path.

Comma butterfly: © Tim Preston

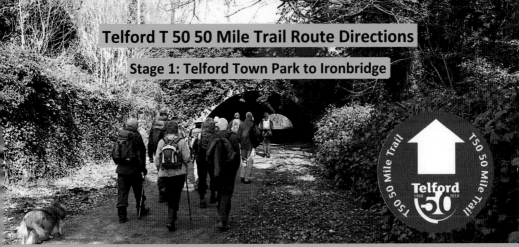

1:1 **Town Park to Woodside. Stage One is the longest on the Trail, 10 .1 miles total. The route description is divided into two equal sections, each 5 miles.**

This Stage starts at the Trail Information Board in Telford Town Centre, easily accessible by bus, train and car. It moves southwards through the Town Park using established paths such as the Silkin Way, the South Telford Way and the South Telford Heritage Trail. The trail then passes through the edge of Madeley and into one of the new housing estates at Aqueduct to reach the picturesque Little Dawley pools and woods. It then crosses Rough Park with lovely views across Telford and ends at the bus shelter on Woodside Avenue, where there are frequent buses back to the Town Centre.

① Town Park to the Ruined Windmill along The Silkin Way 2 miles.

From the Information Centre walk a few yards to the picnic tables behind the old chapel. Take the path just to the left of the lake parallel to the tarmac road,you should see a large Information Board about the Trail marking the star of the Trail here.

Waiting for the ghost train: Dawley and Stirchley Station

At the end of the path turn right onto the tarmac road, continue with Dark Lane car park on your left and rugby club on your right. Just past the rugby club turn left, go down the path and after about 100 yards turn right to follow *The Silkin Way.* After about 500 yards turn right and continue on the Silkin Way, a disused railway line

Pass the old **Dawley and Stirchley station platform** and you soon leave the town park by an archway, turn around and look diagonally half left to see **The Aqueduct**. After another 6 to 8 minutes pass through a short tunnel to reach a junction with a path by a **ruined windmill**.At the windmill (pictured right) take the right branch to leave the Silkin Way which you will rejoin in 6 miles.

② Windmill to Little Dawley Pools 1.2 miles.

Go down a short slope past a lake on your right with a view of an imposing old building on the poolside edge, the historic C16th Madeley Court Manor House, now a hotel. Go past the lake on your right and immediately after the **Madeley Court Hotel** buildings turn right through a gate, walk along a dirt track till you come to the **Madeley Court Hotel access road,** cross over and go straight on. (If you have time to look at the Manor House, which is on your right before you cross the access road, there's an explanatory blue plaque on the Gate House Wall.) Walk straight on over some unmade ground for about 80 yards and turn right at a metal barrier and small metal bridge, cross the bridge and follow a path which goes between two balancing pools. Pass through a gate onto a broad track and turn left. After a minute or so turn right under an arch and below a road bridge. Walk past a row of houses and turn left into a housing estate.

Follow the road round to the left, don't turn right into Willow Bank but follow the road **Gittens Drive** round to the end, 4 minutes or so and reach a main road (40mph sign). Cross the road (island in centre of the road) and take the path immediately opposite.

Walk to the end of the footpath and reach another road. Cross this road onto a footpath signed **Castle Pools.** The path shortly reaches a junction of paths, take the second on the left (not the Ironbridge Way) and follow the track closest to the lake with a number of fishing platforms, on your right. This pool, one of a series of **Little Dawley Pools,** is called **Wide Waters Pool.** There is a large free public car park here for visitors.

Little Dawley to Rough Park Way 0.8 miles

At the end of the lake carry straight on into woods. You soon reach a path junction, take the slight left fork. Turn left at the next path junction, follow this path which passes under electricity wires. Walk past another pool on the right. Carry straight on at the next junction. Just after the pool turn left.

Go right at the next junction and after about 20 yards turn left with another pool on the right, walking past the boardwalk to the right to go straight on passing two benches commenorating two local councillors.

At the next junction turn left and after about 70 yards turn right, following the *South Telford Heritage Trail.* Follow the path through a bridge under a road and go straight on leaving the woods to reach a disused railway line. Cross the line over a stiles either side. About 100 yards or so after the railway tracks you reach a path crossroads with a bench, (unfortunately this area is used illegally by trail bike riders and this short section of path can be very muddy). The bench is a good place for a water stop; turn right to join Rough Park Way.

4   Rough Park Way to Woodside Avenue bus stop 1.2miles

This section of the trail can be a good spot to look for meadow and woodland flowers, fungi,insects and birds. Walk along Rough Park Way track with the Woodside estate up to your left, just visible across the fields. The wide path here has been newly surfaced.

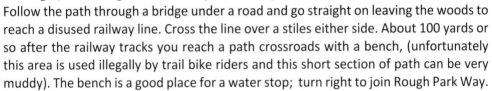

After about a quarter of a mile the path goes through a gate by two houses on your left and does a little twist to the left by crossing a road and then turns right along a track. After the twist carry straight on ignoring paths to the left and right. There is a small stream down to the right and the railway line beyond that. About half a mile after the footpath junction turn left into *Oilhouse Coppice*, follow the path up hill for several minutes, going up steps and then continuing ahead, (ignore the path and steps to the right and later a track to the left).Carry straight on until you reach a picnic table at the top of the path.

Turn left at the picnic table and follow the path through a gate shortly reaching some houses on the left. The path which is now tarmac swings round to the left, cross the road and take the footpath opposite, follow the path until you reach the *Woodside ring road (bus stops here)*.

Telford Bus Station is a short walk from the trail start near the Town Park Information Centre. Stage 1 can be split into two equal sections of 5 miles each: Town Park to Woodside and Woodside to Ironbridge. The bus shelter on Woodside Avenue is the halfway point with frequent buses to and from the Town Centre.

Buses via Madeley Bus Station connect with most of Telford. From there it is a short walk to join or leave the trail at Madeley Court. You can also access the trail easily and return to the Town Centre by buses from Brookside Avenue, walking via the junction of Southall Rd and the Silkin Way.

After leaving the Town Park the only facilities directly on this first part of the trail are at Madeley Court Hotel. It is open to non residents and there is a pleasant lakeside bar where you can sit outside in the summer.

The Golden Ball PH at point 6 on Stage1 is open all day, there are many good pubs on the riverside section between Coalport and Ironbridge and cafes at the YHA in Coalport and at Maws Craft Centre, where there are also free public toilets and a seating area.

Contains Ordnance Survey data © Crown copyright and database right 2017

For downloadable map and gpx files in both clockwise and anticlockwise directions go to: www.telfordt5050miletrail.org.uk

Stage 1: Town Park to Ironbridge

1:2

Woodside to Ironbridge 4.9 miles. Stage One is the longest on the trail, just over 10 miles in total. The route description is divided into two equal parts, each a walk of 5 miles.

This part of Stage 1 starts at the bus shelter on Woodside Avenue, where there are frequent buses from the Town Centre. From there it goes through The Beeches and Lodge Fields Nature Reserves from where you will enjoy extensive views of the Ironbridge Gorge. The route continues through the upper parts of Ironbridge, then down to The River Severn via Lloyds Coppice Woods, The Silkin Way disused railway line, Coalport and Jackfield passing major historical sites on the way to finish in the World Heritage Site of Ironbridge by crossing the famous Iron Bridge.

5 Woodside Bus Shelter to the Golden Ball Pub 1.5 Miles

You are now facing the ***Woodside Estate***, turn right at the bus shelter and quickly take a path to the right away from the road, which becomes a narrow way between woodland and fields. Turn left onto a tarmac road, (**Beech Road)**. After 100 yds or so you reach a house, take the narrow fenced path on the right, pass through a gate and continue straight on with a field on your left. At the end and turn right onto a lane, an old finger post is marked "To Ironbridge". Walk about 300 yards and take a track that branches to the right away from **Orchard Lane,** after a few yards go through the entrance gate to the ***Beeches Field Local Nature Reserve*** on the right.

Look up to see buzzards soaring, a common sight here. Follow the path through the reserve, passing a pool on the left. There is a bench at the top, a lovely spot for a brief rest; admire the views of the Black Country in the far distance.

Continue up and leave the Beeches LNR at a gate and turn right, there is a house on the left. After about 150 yards you can see the **White Horse** pub ahead of you, there is a finger post pointing left into **Lodge Field Nature Reserve,** take the signed path towards and into Lodge Field. Enjoy the views of the wooded **Severn Gorge,** meadow flowers and bird life. Follow the clear track on the left to the bottom, through a gate and turn right. Leave Lodge Field.

There is a fingerpost here. Walk straight down. When you reach a road turn left and after about 40 yards turn right into **Belle Vue.** The road becomes an alley, then a narrow lane called **Hillside;** continue ignoring roads off to the right and left. You are now in **Ironbridge.** The road is gently undulating with lovely views to the right – the **River Severn** can be seen below as it moves into Ironbridge. You soon reach a road by a house with a lovely name, **The Wedge of Cheese**, bear slightly right and look for a house on the left with a plaque indicating the birthplace of a famous local hero. Carry on to the main **Madeley Rd**. Cross over carefully as there is a sharp blind bend to the right. The house at this junction used to be a public house where the bodies of the Madeley Nine miners were put after the accident. **The Nine Men of Madeley Trail** tells their story. Walk to the **Golden Ball pub** directly ahead.

⑥ The Golden Ball PH to Coalport & Jackfield Memorial Bridge 1.9 miles

Keep the pub on the right and walk down **Wesley Road** to its end, after about 500 yards just before a junction, go left through a gate with a finger post signed to Blist's Hill and enter **Lloyds Coppice** woods**.** Continue on the clear woodland path, past a path junction from your right and shortly after you come to a finger post signed to Blists Hill, turn sharp left and go up a long flight of steps which bears right and becomes quite steep, at the top is a path junction, follow the finger post directions pointing down to Blist' Hill to the left . Go down past a garden fence on your right, through a narrow gate to emerge past two houses onto a main road, **Legges Way.** Cross into the car park opposite at the back of the **Blist's Hill Museum** (workers entrance).Turn left following the finger post sign, then left again after a few yards to go through a long tunnel.

Follow the **Silkin Way** to Coalport along the disused **London & North Western Railway line**. Beneath you lies the main Telford sewer. You pass underneath the **Hay Inclined Plane**, ignore the first path down to the right and turn right opposite a bench and gate, go past the **Coalport Village Hall** to join a road, opposite a bus stop and **Coalport China Museum**. Cross the road , go over a bridge and turn right to follow a canalside path. At the end, go left over the **Jackfield & Coalport Memorial Bridge**, a unique First World War Memorial. Before you cross look back to view the full length of the **Hay Inclined Plane,** used to bring loaded tugboats down to the canal/river wharf for eventual onward transport to Bristol. The **Tar Tunnel** entrance is across the canal to the right.

7 The Memorial Bridge to The Iron Bridge 1.5 miles

Cross the bridge, turn right along the river but pause to look at the door of **The Boat** public house showing record floodwater levels. After 50 yards bear left and follow the massive old wall of the old **Maws Works.** At the end of the wall carry straight across into an alleyway which ends behind the **Half Moon** public house. Go past the Half Moon and take the footpath right, closest to the river. You will see Jackfield church in front of you. There is lovely tile artwork by local children by the picnic area up the

steps on the left near the end of the path. Walk up and bear slight right onto the road, keep the chuch on your left (wonderful craft work by local people inside) to reach the **Ironbridge Gorge Tile Museum.** Turn right walk along the road to a level crossing gate (the Great Western Railway ran to Paddington from here). Go straight on to the left of the level crossing, through a gate and along the path, a disused railway line with ruined station platforms. After half a mile you enter a large car park with the Iron Bridge clearly in view ahead right. Turn right to cross the Iron Bridge into Ironbridge.

Stage 1: Town Park to Ironbridge 10.1 Miles.

Telford Town Park Information Centre, near to where the Trail begins, is a short walk from the train and bus stations and signposted from the town centre. There are free public toilets in the Information Centre and an open air cafe and picnic area is available.

Buses from Ironbridge to Telford Town Centre and to Bridgnorth, Brosleley, Madeley, Much Wenlock and Shrewsbury all depart from the car park by the Museum of the Gorge near Dale End. Some buses, but not all, also depart from the bridge, please check with the bus company website.

There are free public toilets at Maws Craft Centre, Ironbridge Market Square and next to Dale End bus station. Pubs and cafes on the route are shown. There is a wide choice of facilities near the Town Park and in Ironbridge.

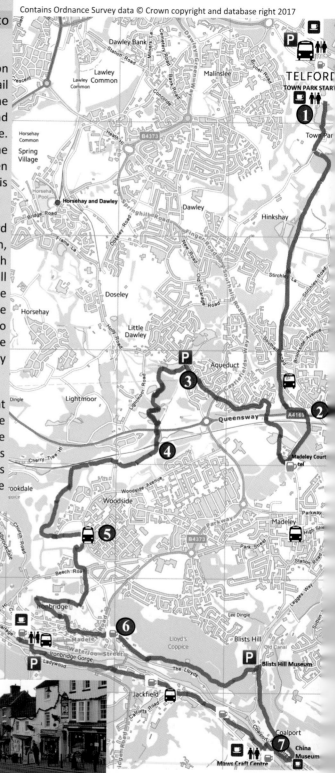

Contains Ordnance Survey data © Crown copyright and database right 2017

2 *A lovely walk, 4.3 miles, through woodlands and open country with extensive views and lots of history. NB There are three series of steep steps in the woods.*

① Ironbridge to The Rotunda 0.8 miles

From the Iron Bridge (there's a bus stop next to the war memorial by the bridge) walk downhill alongside the river to the **Ironbridge Gorge Museum of the River** *(bus station)*. Opposite the Teddy Bear Shop by the Co-op turn right into **Paradise**. The lane climbs quite steeply, you are heading for the best view in Ironbridge. After about 200 yards take the path to the right and carry on to a wooden gate, go through the gate and at the footpath junction turn right signposted **'Rotunda'**, this path leads you to the bottom of the famous Rotunda steps. *(However, if 173 steep steps are a challenge too far, go straight on at the finger post. At a gate turn left onto Church Rd to rejoin the route at the church).*

Walk on for a few hundred yards , past steps on the right and then climb the long flight of steps on the left to enjoy the spectacular views of the whole of the Ironbridge Gorge and Coalbrookdale from the top of the **Rotunda**, a trail highlight.

② The Rotunda to Loamhole Dingle 1.1 miles

Get your breath back and continue along the summit path; don't be tempted to explore the gaps in the trees to your right, it's a sheer (and fast)drop down to Ironbridge. Walk through the woods, at the finger post bear left to Paradise, then slight right to Church Rd at the next sign post. Go through a gate and cross over **Church Rd.** Follow the path left through the gate signed to *Woodside*. These woods are rich in wildlife with 'seat sculptures' and good views. The woods are managed by *Severn Gorge Countryside Trust*. The paths are *Sabbath Walks,* devised by C19th industrialists to keep the work force out of the pubs on Sundays!

Follow finger posts signs to **Church Road**. Go down the steps, steep left and left fork down to a gate to exit onto Church Rd opposite the church. There are good views from the church, and if open, interesting memorials to local heroes and the Darby family; so enter the graveyard, turn right then rejoin the road and continue downhill. At the end of **Church Rd**, cross the main road, turn right and immediately left down the slip road into *The Museum of Iron* complex past a 'no entry sign'. Go past the museum entrance. There are public toilets to your left. A restaurant is due to open here 2019. Cross the car park to a no exit sign, take the exit signed *"Darby Houses."* There are picnic tables on the right. As you walk under the *Coalbrookdale viaduct* turn right. The *Upper Furnace Pool* once provided back up for the ironwork's furnace pools; now it's a wildlife area. Cross the road ahead and take the path underneath the arch beneath the wooden bridge to enter woodland.

NB. Museum car park closes an hour after the museum , 4pm in summer, closed Mondays in winter. If closed cross the road at the end of Church Road and turn right along the main road past the Coalbrookdale Inn. After a couple of hundred yards take the road on the left and pass the Coalbrookdale Community Centre on your left, and join the route a few yards on by crossing the road and turning right to the arch beneath the wooden bridge

3 Loamhole Dingle to Leasowes Farm 0.8 miles

You are now in **Loamhole Dingle**. Cross the little bridge and follow a wooden walkway with the stream on your left. Keep to the path to the right, the one just by the stream can flood. Continue for about half a mile, over board walks, some steps up and down. Cross a bridge and continue with the stream now on your right. Climb the flight of steps until you reach the gateway at the top. Turn right. Follow the track through a  gateway into **Lydebrook Dingle.** Climbing more steep steps, you will now follow the **Shropshire Way** (orange waymarks with a buzzard symbol) for a few miles. You will reach a path junction with waymarks, turn left before a final flight of steps. At the top cross the stile into a field, aim for a gate flanked by two white pillars to the left of a house, **Leasowes Farm**, and turn left onto a road.

4 Leasowes Farm to Little Wenlock 1.6 miles

You have now left the woods behind you and the nature of the walk changes to more open country. As you follow the road, there are good views of The Wrekin to the right. Turn right at the junction through a gate onto another road. Cross the bridge over the **Ironbridge Bypass**, there are good views of **Wenlock Edge** to the left. Continue to follow the quiet lane and after a few minutes take the left turn. Walk past **Moor Farm Cottage** and immediately after turn right over a stile by a large metal gate. Cross the field diagonally left, due West, aim for the last left in a line of four large oak trees half way along the field fence in the distance in front of you. **NB If using OS maps, please note there is a fence shown on the map at the oak tree point, this fence no longer exists**. At the oak tree turn right and follow the fence to the top of the field. At the next fence climb the stile and turn right. **The path across the next field no longer follows the line on the OS map, take care here**. The new right of way is follow the field boundary fence/hedge keeping it on your right all the way. Cross a stile at the top of the field, turn right onto a track which eventually becomes **Buildwas Lane.** Enjoy glimpses of the **Breiddens, Welsh** and **Shropshire Hill**s on the far horizon. After a few minutes you pass the sign to **Little Wenlock** to reach a wall with the church on your right. To continue to Wellington via the **Shropshire Way** turn left. To finish, go straight on, to the crossroads. The **Huntsman** welcomes walkers.

Public transport and facilities: T50 50 Mile Trail Stage 2 to Little Wenlock

Contains Ordnance Survey data © Crown copyright and database right 2017

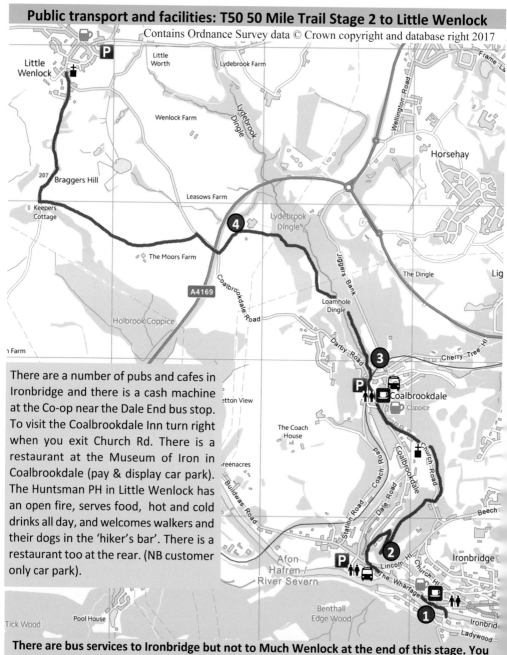

There are a number of pubs and cafes in Ironbridge and there is a cash machine at the Co-op near the Dale End bus stop. To visit the Coalbrookdale Inn turn right when you exit Church Rd. There is a restaurant at the Museum of Iron in Coalbrookdale (pay & display car park). The Huntsman PH in Little Wenlock has an open fire, serves food, hot and cold drinks all day, and welcomes walkers and their dogs in the 'hiker's bar'. There is a restaurant too at the rear. (NB customer only car park).

There are bus services to Ironbridge but not to Much Wenlock at the end of this stage. You could use buses to start at Coalbrookdale and finish on stage 3, either where you cross the B5061 (9 miles), or in Wellington Town Centre (10 miles). The *Gorge Connect* bus service runs on Bank Holiday and Summer weekends only between all the Museum sites, so you might end Stage 1 at Coalport China Museum and finish the next stage at Coalbrookdale,(just under 4 miles); a good idea if you want to visit the museums on route. There's limited free parking at Little Wenlock Village Hall in Wellington Rd (see displayed notices).

Stage 3: Little Wenlock to Wellington

3

This most rural and scenic 7.7 mile stage of the trail starts in the village of Little Wenlock and meanders through the woods at the south side of The Wrekin before climbing to the 407m high summit with outstanding views (optional – the highest point of the trail) then uphill over The Ercall Nature Reserve through more woods and into the market town of Wellington with a wide range of shops, facilities and excellent transport links.

If starting from the village, walk down Church Lane, directly opposite The Huntsman

1 Little Wenlock to Wenlocks Wood 2.2 miles

Turn down **Witchwell Lane,** opposite *St Lawrence Church,* and follow the lane around to the right. Go through the gate ahead, turn right through a second gate and follow the right field edge. This is part of the *'Little Wenlock Bench Walk'.* Go through a gate, cross a footbridge and continue to follow the wire fence. Go through the next gate past the bench of David Hutchison, the late former Chief Executive of Wrekin Council, after whom the Hutchison Way was named. Go through the gate onto **Spout Lane** and turn left.

Walk down the lane for about three quarters of a mile until you come to a house on the left *"The Firs".* Turn right opposite the house. Walk straight ahead along the woodland path. At the gate, cross the stile and follow the hedgerow on the right. Cross the stile and continue walking past the farm towards and then into and through *Wenlocks Wood.* There is a bluebell display here in early May, you may spot deer here too.

② Wenlocks Wood to The Wrekin Summit 1.6 miles

At the edge of the woods, turn left at the public footpath sign, using large rocks as a stile (the cross piece has gone). Walk along the left edge of the field following the wire fence. Continue along the left edge of the next field. Go over the stile at the end of the field. Join the footpath after the stile and follow it to the right. Continue on this path taking you around the bottom of the Wrekin, passing the map of the area.

Where the path forks, take the left path up the hill, passing the **Halfway House** cafe with beautiful views of The Ercall from their garden, it is often open for light refreshments. Follow the main track as it bends to the left to go up the Wrekin (note the short waymarked post, you will turn at the same post on your descent). Continue uphill past information boards about the prehistoric hill fort to the summit of **The Wrekin and the toposcope at 1,335 feet/407 metres.** As the Wrekin can be seen from nearly everywhere in Shropshire you can see nearly all of Shropshire from here and many places beyond, 17 counties in all. It is a highlight well worth the climb.

③ The Wrekin Summit to The Ercall Summit 2.6 miles

From the toposcope (no waymark) retrace your steps down, at the fork keep left. Where the path starts to swing round to the right (waymarked short post) take the small path to the left at the corner. Near the bottom of the path, go around a large tree that has fallen across the path and at the edge of the woods, join the perimeter path and turn right. Follow the path down to join the road and turn right and walk along the edge of the road **(Wrekin Course).**

At the T junction cross the road and cross over a stile towards a **reservoir.** Continue past the large reservoir on your right and keep to the left when the path forks. At the end of the path, turn right onto the wide grassy path. Follow the grassy path to the road and turn left. Walk along the side of the road and turn right through a gate into **The Ercall Wood Nature Reserve.** Follow the path into **Ercall Wood.** Notice the unconformity of the exposed quarry rocks on the left where the Ercall Granophyte and the Wrekin Quartzite meet. Stay on the central path, which passes just to the right of a large rock.

Continue uphill and eventually, where the path divides, take the bigger left path and continue straight up the steep ascent of *The Ercall.* You next reach a path junction where the main **Shropshire Way** turns right; you don't.

If you follow the Shropshire Way here you will miss one of the highlights of the trail, namely the viewpoint from The Ercall. Continue straight on (and up) and you quickly reach another path junction where you turn left. Note this point as you will be returning very close to here on your way down. In a few minutes you will meet a fence which runs along the *summit of The Ercall.* Do not attempt to cross the fence as the dangerous drop is substantial. Walk along with the fence on your left and enjoy the views of The Wrekin and elsewhere. After about 70 yards turn right at a path junction. Carry on uphill and you will soon come close to the point where you turned up the final part of the hill, continue straight on. Start to descend with lovely views to the right. These woods are noted for flowers, fungi, birds, butterflies and other insects.

4 The Ercall to Wellington Town Centre 1.3 miles

Continue downhill on the path and then turn left to rejoin the **Shropshire Way.** Turn right where the path gets close to the motorway and continue over the footbridge and along the path. Turn left at the end of the path, **Golf Links Lane** *(underpass),* and follow ithe lane to the end. Cross the **Holyhead Road** at the pedestrian crossing. Turn left and then almost immediately turn right down a footpath. Continue down the footpath, cross the road, **Roseway**, and continue onto the public footpath still on the **Shropshire Way.** Turn left at the road, **Tan Bank.** Turn left and cross **Victoria Road** at the pedestrian island. Continue to the left down **Victoria Road** and turn right into the *Wellington Civic and Leisure Centre*, where there is a cafe and toilets and a large car park. To reach the bus and train station turn right out of *Wellington Leisure Centre* and walk down the pedestrian walkway, **Larkin Way.** (notice the *Peace Garden* on the left). Walk slightly right into the **Pedestrian Zone.** Walk through the **Market Square.** The turning to the *Railway Station* is on the right; follow signs to *Bus Station*.

MAP Stage 3 Little Wenlock to Wellington Transport and Facilities

There is limited car parking (note signs) at Little Wenlock Village Hall and customer only parking at The Hunstman (open all day). The Forest Glen CP below The Wrekin is free but busy at weekends. The Halfway House plans to open the cafe from Summer 2019, hot drinks and limited snacks are available at their outdoor kiosk. There is a cafe at Wellington Library with time limited parking, an unrestricted car park is on the opposite side of the road. There are many shops, cafes and pubs in Wellington town centre.

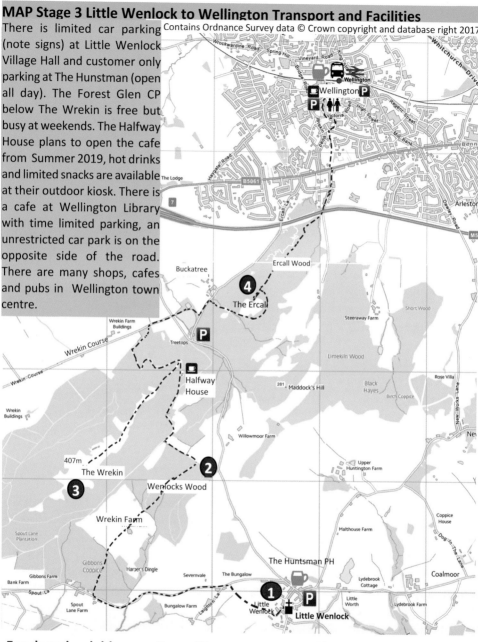

Contains Ordnance Survey data © Crown copyright and database right 2017

For downloadable map & gpx files go to: www.telfordt5050miletrail.org.uk

Little Wenlock has one bus only via Wellington on Tuesdays so you will need to use cars or start this Stage from Coalbrookdale. There are trains to Shrewsbury, Oakengates and Telford and good bus services to Shrewsbury and all parts of Telford from the bus station behind the railway station (both are signed and easily accessible from the Trail.)

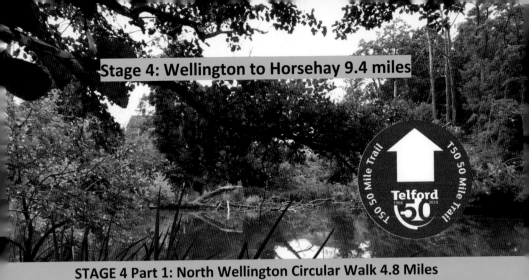

4:1 STAGE 4 Part 1: North Wellington Circular Walk 4.8 Miles

The long Stage 4 is divided into 2 walks of equal length. Part 1 is almost a circular walk, starting and finishing in Wellington town centre.

This varied stage starts in the busy market town of Wellington with interesting green spaces adjacent to residential areas. It is a delightful ramble through the town, woods, local nature reserves and across open spaces. Car drivers and some bus users may opt to start from the Leisure Centre, others from the main rail and bus stations, the route guidance gives both options.

1 Wellington to Dohill Local Nature Reserve 1 mile

With your back to the main door of *Wellington Leisure Centre*, turn right and walk down the pedestrian walkway, **Larkin Way** with the *Peace Garden* on the left. Cross the road into the **Pedestrian Zone** and turn left into **Duke Street**. Walk through the **Market Square.** Pass the turning to the *Railway Station* on the right. (**If starting from the bus or train stations exit via Station Road and turn right, you are now at this point.**) Walk on for 40 yards. Turn left into the small alley, **Ten Tree Croft** before the road bends to the right. A brown plaque marks where cloth was hung in the 1700s. Continue down the alley and turn right along the road, cross over the next road, **Queen Street** and walk up **Charlton Street**. Cross over the larger **Vineyard Road** and turn left. Cross **Vineyard Drive** and continue straight ahead on the path above the road. Turn right into **North Road**, cross the road at the pedestrian crossing and continue up North Road. After passing *St Patrick's Catholic Primary School* on your left turn left into **Deer Park Road**. Continue past a low post with **Shropshire Way** and **T50** waymarks. Walk past the garages on the left and walk between the metal barriers to turn into **Barnet Close**. Continue along Barnet Close and turn right into **Cound Close,** at the end cross **Severn Drive.**

② Dothill Local Nature Reserve (LNR) to Apley Woods 1.1 mile

Leave the **Shropshire Way** here to enter *Dothill LNR* walking to the left of the footpath towards the wooden fence. Note:- no path here. Continue on the grassy swathe with *Dothill Pool* on your right to cross **Severn Drive** again. Walk up **Morville Drive** to the end and go through the gate to re-enter *Dothill LNR*. Note the plaques of the *50 Tree Trail* as you walk through the Nature Reserve. Go down the steps and carry straight on. At the fork in the path bear right. At the next junction turn right when you meet a stoned path. At the T junction turn right to rejoin the **Shropshire Way.** Continue along the path with T Lake on the right. There are picnic tables here. Bear right to continue on the **Shropshire Way.** Continue on the tarmac path and recross **Severn Drive** at the pedestrian crossing place. Continue on the footpath and bear left, still following the **Shropshire Way** for a short distance. At the next junction, continue straight on ahead, leaving the **Shropshire Way** here. Turn right at the road and walk up **Harley Close.** Turn left into **The Savannahs, Severn Drive**. Turn right into the **The Savannahs, Whitchurch Rd.**

③ Apley Woods to Leegomery 1.4 miles

Cross the road as the road bends to the right, turn left **uphill** onto the footpath and cycle track. Turn left to cross the foot bridge. Continue along the path until it meets a road and turn left. Shortly after, turn left through a pedestrian gate at *Apley Home Farm*. Almost immediately turn right and go through the kissing gate onto the path that runs along the boundary fence on the right. Continue along this path and go through a gap in the fence on the right into *Apley Woods. Apley Pool* is visible in front of the gap. Turn right again, onto the path. Continue along the path and where the path forks, take the left fork. Turn left at the beginning of the green open space and walk along the path towards an information board. *Apley Pool* is on the left. Turn 90 degrees right at the information board and cross the grassy space towards the steps at the far end. Go up the 4 sets of steps passing the stone seats and at the top turn right. There are lovely drifts of snowdrops here at the end of January.

Shortly after, go down a few steps and continue ahead. At a 5 way junction take the first path on the left, passing an information board and walk down the wonderful *Yew Avenue* and at the end turn left. Continue on the path and where it divides, turn right towards the kissing gate. Go through the kissing gate and continue along the straight path, part of the **Silkin Way,** with impressive lime trees on both sides. Continue along the path, going under the road (has a bus stop). Continue walking straight ahead with the shops, including the fish and chip shop, on your right.

4 Leegomery Community Centre to Wellington High Street 1.3 miles

Turn right immediately after the *Leegomery Community Centre*. Take the path that bends to the left past the finger post which marks the beginning of the **Ironbridge Way.** Take the left fork after the Ironbridge Way finger post. Continue and turn left to join the next path and where the stone wall ends, turn right across the access road onto the foot and cycle path. Stay on the main foot and cycle path with *Leegomery Pool* on your left. Turn right before the end of the pool, opposite the shallow steps which descend to the pool. (Take care here, lots of paths).Turn left into **Catterick Close.** Turn right after *house number 7* and continue through the *underpass*. Continue on the main path, bearing right as the slope eases off. Walk straight for about half a mile and cross the *footbridge*. Turn left where the path meets **College Lane.** Cross **Exeter Drive** and continue up **College Lane.** Continue straight on into **Roslyn Road** and walk along, passing *Wrekin College Cricket Pavilion* on your left. Turn left into **Albert Road.** Walk along **Albert Road** and turn right into **Constitution Hill.** Walk down the hill passing the *Union Free Church* on your left. At the bottom of **Constitution Hill** cross **King Street** at the zebra crossing and walk straight ahead up **Victoria Road.**

There is easy access to the train and bus stations here to your right. If continuing to Part 2 stay on this side of **Victoria Rd** and continue up hill passing *Wellington Medical Practice* on the left. Turn left into **High Street** at the old *Chad Valley Toy Factory* building where Part 2 starts. Look for the CV in the decorative work on the front of the building.

Contains Ordnance Survey data © Crown copyright and database right 2017

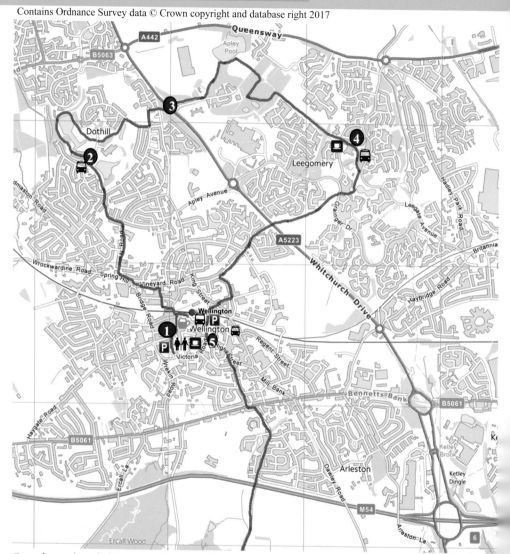

For downloadable map & gpx files go to: www.telfordt5050miletrail.org.uk

Buses from Telford to Wellington Bus Station include No, 7, X4, X5, 15, 4, 16. The No 15 passes close to the trail in Dothill. Please check on transport websites as routes and bus numbers may change at short notice. There are buses to Wellington and Telford town centres and a fish and chip shop too, near stage point 4 in Leegomery. Facilities are plentiful in Wellington but sparse after you cross the B5061 Holyhead Road.

There are bus services to and from Shrewsbury from Wellington. There are trains between Shrewsbury, Wellington, Oakengates and Telford Central railway stations.

Stage 4: Wellington to Horsehay 9 .4 miles

STAGE 4 Part 2: Wellington to Horsehay 4.6 Miles
The long Stage 4 is divided into 2 walks of almost equal length.

4:2 *This very varied walk starts in the busy market town of Wellington with excellent rail and bus transport links, good facilities and many car parks. There are fascinating green spaces adjacent to residential areas, delightful rambles by pools, through woods and wide open spaces with panoramic views, former mining areas returned to nature and even a golf course near Horsehay Steam Railway. A good stage for spotting birds and deer.*

5 **High Street to The White Cottage at the end of Limekiln Lane 1.2 miles**

There is easy access from the train and bus stations. If starting this secton of the stage from the rail station cross the railway bridge and then **exit via Platform 1 (the Wolverhampton side) into Victoria Road and turn right.** Continue up hill along **Victoria Rd** passing *Wellington Medical Practice* on the left. Turn left into **High Street** at the old *Chad Valley Toy Factory* building where Part 2 starts. Look for the CV in the decorative work on the front of the building. Starting at the *Old Chad Valley Toy Factory* walk along **High Street**, away from Wellington town centre and at the roundabout cross over, past the shops on your right, to walk along **New Church Road**, passing a blue plaque to mark the birthplace of the painter Cecil Lawson on the left. Continue straight on past the entrance to **Christ Church** to meet **Holyhead Road** (the old Roman Road, *Watling Street*). Turn left and cross at the pedestrian crossing. Turn right and immediately left into **Limekiln Lane**. Walk down Limekiln Lane past *Short Wood Sports and Outdoor Centre* on the left. Continue straight past the walking and cycling sign. Continue up Limekiln Lane, **under the M54** towards *Steeraway*. 30 yards after the *Steeraway sign* turn right at the stile, which is just before *The White Cottage*.

Follow the path to the T junction at the top and turn right to join the path that marks the edge of **Limekiln Wood**. 25 yards along, turn left uphill onto another path. Continue along this path, at the grassy clearing you can find spotted orchids in June. On the left there is an open shaft of one of the *lime kilns* that give the wood its name. Turn right where a metal barrier crosses the path. After 20 yards take the left fork. Continue until you reach a stile. Cross the stile and continue on the path through the field and pass **Limekiln Pool** which will be on your right. Here you can clearly see that you are walking on an old tramway.

Keep alert and move quietly and you may glimpse the deer herd that wanders freely through the woods and over open ground in the this section. Continue along the path across the next field. Cross the stile into **Short Wood**. Keep straight on then walk across the forest track, continue straight up over the stile and follow the path, which ascends steeply. Cross the next stile. Take the right fork after the stile. Stay on the path as it bends first to the left and then to the right. At the end of the path turn right onto a wide stone path, created through the area where the recent open-cast mining took place. Follow this stone path for about half a mile passing three information boards. The stone path continues between wooden railings. At the T junction turn left and continue to the end to turn left through a gate onto a lane.

Walk along the lane to reach New Works, passing the entrance *to* **Smalley Hill Nature Reserve** on the right.

7   New Works to Horsehay 1.9 miles

Turn left into **New Works Lane t**owards Wellington. Continue along the Lane and at the last bungalow on the left, turn right down the multi-user trail, the *Trundle.* Walk down the Trundle, at the end turn right and continue along the busy **Dawley Road**, ignoring all roads to the right. Just after the *children's play area*, bear right onto the cycle and footpath. Continue straight ahead and cross the footbridge. Cross the road and take the bridleway straight ahead. Continue on this as it turns left after the houses and follow the fence along the edge of the wood until it turns left. Here keep straight on to ascend the bank.

Cross in front of the *tee off* (be mindful of golfers) and turn right onto the gravel path passing a bench on your left. Follow the path and turn left at the low post. Continue straight down the gravel path. At the junction of paths, take the descending gravel path and continue along the foot of the slope to where the path comes to an end. Bear left on a grassy path , past a litter bin, towards a house to reach a kissing gate and turn left onto the lane. Continue on the road, turn right at the crossroads and walk down the lane designated 'unsuitable for HGVs' passing the houses of *Spring Village.*

At the bottom of the lane, cross the little road and take the public footpath straight ahead. There are picnic tables here. At the end of the footpath turn left. Horsehay Pool is on your left and on your right rows of cottgages, built for the iron workers of the C18th. The fish and chip shop *Cod Father* is on the right as you join the main road. Turn left here to reach the *Telford Steam Railway*. (The *Railway cafe* is open Sundays April/ Oct) and to continue walking on Stage 5 of the Trail. Turn right and continue down Bridge Road for the bus stop near the Village Hall, for buses to Telford or to Coalbrookdale, Ironbridge and Shrewsbury: the stop name on timetables is Horsehay Farm Lane.

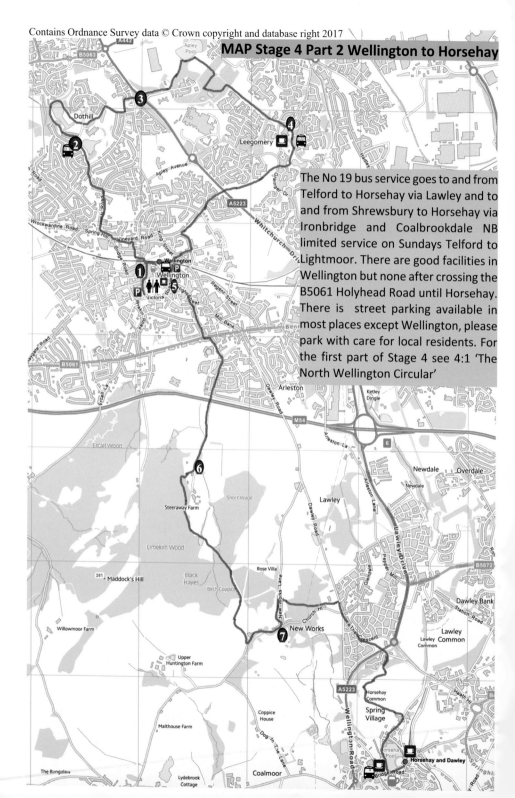

The No 19 bus service goes to and from Telford to Horsehay via Lawley and to and from Shrewsbury to Horsehay via Ironbridge and Coalbrookdale NB limited service on Sundays Telford to Lightmoor. There are good facilities in Wellington but none after crossing the B5061 Holyhead Road until Horsehay. There is street parking available in most places except Wellington, please park with care for local residents. For the first part of Stage 4 see 4:1 'The North Wellington Circular'

Stage 5: Horsehay to Oakengates 5.1 miles

5 *This stage starts by passing the Telford Steam Railway. It then uses some of the Ironbridge Way and goes through some of Telford's newest developments with views of The Wrekin over the tops of the housing estates. The sanctuary of Paddock Mound gives some lovely views before the trail moves through some more new development prior to reaching Oakengates station with trains to and from Shrewsbury, Wolverhampton and Birmingham.*

Horsehay to Lawley 1.3 miles

Walk along **Bridge Road** with *Horsehay Pool* on your left. Turn left at the first lamp post and almost immediately right at the brick wall. Continue on the path past *Telford Steam Railway.* Cross the access road to Spring Village and continue ahead over the railway bridge. Turn left onto Fence Road. You are now on the Ironbridge Way, IBW. (There is a *cafe at Railway House*, open on Sundays between April and October). Continue on Fence Road along the Restricted Byway. Turn left at the road, (**Dawley Road**). Cross the road near the '*Ironstone*' sign. Take the tarmac path in the direction of **Newdale**. Continue keeping the hedge on your right to where eventually you pass the school playing fields on your left. Ignore the path coming from the right. Shortly after, the path

bends to the right (notice the wrought iron railings on the right). Cross the narrow road at the zebra crossing and turn left. At the end of the buildings, you turn right towards the traffic lights.

Cross the road at the pelican crossing in front of the building with the Morrisons sign.Continue down the paved area towards the building of **Haygate Veterinary Centre.** Turn right at **Market Street Cafe**, which is part of **Morrisons** (there are toilets here.) Pass the main entrance to Morrisons on your right and continue on to the T junction. Turn left and continue downhill on **Gresham Drive**,

passing *Lawley Village Day Nursery*. Turn left at the roundabout and soon after, cro the road and turn right onto a footpath before the houses. Continue on the footpat passing through a gateway. Bear left at the lake and continue on the footpath.Follc the path as it bends to the right with another path coming in from the left, still followi the **Ironbridge Way (IBW).**

② Lawley to the Holyhead Road 2 miles

At the next T junction, turn left to leave IBW here. At the next road, turn right and wa downhill on the footpath. At the middle of the second pool on the left, take the footpa and steps to the right. Take the path down to the left. Cross the footbridge and tu right. (notice the *Grade 2 listed old tramway bridge* on the right) Turn left onto t footpath and go up the steps. Turn left at the top of the steps to rejoin the **Ironbrid Way.** Continue along the **IBW**. Continue on the footpath as it bears to the right ne to the **M54.** At the road, **Waterloo Road**, turn left. Go through the *underpass* a after 100 yards turn right. Walk along the concrete path and, 25 yards past t *children's playground*, take the faint path to the left. Continue on the path and whe the houses begin, take the grassy path straight ahead. Continue on the path and at t cross road of paths, go straight ahead. At the end of the path, cross the road and w ahead into the road,

Snowdrop Meadow.
Turn right at the top of **Snowdrop Meadow**. Walk along on the footpath, turn left and walk down **Red Lees.** When you reach steps on the right, turn right and go up the steps. There is a large *interpretation board* here about *Paddock Mound.*

Turn left at the top of the steps onto the top of **Paddock Mound.** There are picnic tables here and wonderful views of **The Wrekin.** Continue round to the left and take the steps down. Turn right at the bottom of the steps and continue on the path. At the fork in the path turn left and go down the steps. Continue

on the path, past a section of the old canal and continue along the gravel path. Go through the gate at the end of the footpath, cross the **Holyhead Road**. (bus stop here)

3   Holyhead Road to Oakengates 1.8 miles

Turn right along the road and bear left down **Beverley Road** by the **Mauchak Indian Restaurant**. Immediately after the Mauchak car park, turn left down a wide footpath. Continue down the footpath and turn right onto a paved path. Immediately turn left and then keep right onto a gravel path after the playground, towards the houses. At the end of the path, cross the road and take the gravel footpath ahead, which is slightly to the left. At the T junction turn right. At the next T junction turn left. Keep right as you pass the metal grid on the left. Just before the metal sided bridge, turn sharply right, up the gravel path (do not cross the bridge.) Continue to the end of the path and at the road, (**Beveley Road**), turn left. Continue along the pavement and walk past **the Compasses Inn** on the left with **Jenko's Mongolian Barbecue** behind the Inn. Walk through the **underpass** which is on the line of the **Roman Road**, **Watling Street**. Continue up the road, then continue straight on down **Hartshill**, where there's a No bus stop . Cross the road at the pedestrian crossing by **Wombridge Primary School**, turn left and immediately after the school playground, turn right onto the footpath. Continue on the footpath and turn left at the road, **Vicar Street**. At the end of Vicar Street, cross the road, **Charlton Street** and continue straight on.

Cross the next road and continue straight ahead along the footpath between the houses. Keep left as the path descends towards more houses. At the T junction turn right and cross the bridge to continue on the route. Alternatively you can access the **railway station** and Oakengates at this point.

Map Stage 5: Horsehay to Oakengates

There are lots of occasions for snack stops on this stage as you pass many shops, pubs and cafes on the way starting with The Codfather 'chippie' in Horsehay. There are a number of pubs , coffee shops and take aways in Oakengates. There are large free car parks near to the railway station and The Place Theatre .

Bus No.19 stops near the roundabout at the bottom of Bridge Rd at the start of the Stage in Horsehay. There are bus services to Lawley and there is a bus stop on Holyhead Rd near Paddock Mound in Ketley. Oakengates bus station has services to Telford and Wellington town centres and many other places via buses No 4, 5, 5A, 7, 13 and 15.

The rail station has direct trains to Telford Central, Wolverhamton, Birmingham,Wellington, and Shrewsbury

Contains Ordnance Survey data © Crown copyright and database right 201

Ketley Paddock Mound has one of Britain's most beautiful bus shelters with scenes of local wildlife painted by Shrewsbury artist Fran O' Boyle. He also painted a large 24m mural about the history of Ketley, on the wall at the back of Ketley Community Centre: turn left at the bus shelter if you want to take a quick look.

6 *Starting at the public footbridge over the railway line next to Oakengates Train Station, this six mile stage meanders through a mix of residential and green areas before moving out into more open countryside towards the conspicuous Lilleshall Hill and its Monument. NB No facilities after Oakengates.*

① Oakengates Station to The Nabb 1.4 miles

If following on from Stage 5 this stage begins at the public footbridge over the railway line next to Oakengates Station. If starting at the station, turn left through the exit from platform 2 onto a rough track. Then turn left again after a short while onto the public footbridge. Cross the line and carry on straight ahead.

Cross the main road (**Station Rd**) and turn left, then right onto **Canongate**. Follow this road and shortly after the bridge over the dual carriageway, take a footpath to the right, following the **NCN55 cycle trail route**. Follow this path, turning left up steps after about 200 yards, through a picnic area with a view of The Wrekin. Continue along this path through a wooded area to a T-junction and turn left downhill, through a gate to the road. Turn left along the road, then right into **Eaton Crescent** and then left along **Athol Drive**. At the end of Athol Drive, turn right, then through the opening by the 5-barred gate ahead. Keep to the right-hand path and turn right through the woods. When you reach an open area turn hard left back into the woods. Follow the path downhill to a stile onto a road (**West St**). Turn left, then cross the road when opposite **Albion St**. Continue along **West St** then fork right along **Hilton Terrace** continuing straight on towards **The Nabb**.

❷ The Nabb to St Georges Rd via Wrockwardine Woods 1.7 miles

Continue along **The Nabb**. When you reach a junction, ignore the footpath to your right, but stay on The Nabb by bearing slightly right following the restricted byway sign and passing house numbers 94-92. Continue along the track ignoring the first right turn. At the next junction bear right then turn immediate left into the *Wrockwardine Woods* through a metal half-circle kissing gate. Keep on the main footpath. At a T-junction turn right. Continue to follow the well-trodden path, then turn right at a major junction of paths. Follow this path, soon passing an open area with picnic benches. Fork left just beyond the open area. Follow this path, eventually dropping down to the main track, turn hard left onto the main track.

Continue for some distance through the woods of *Cockshutt Piece* ignoring a path joining from the left. Go through a gate, bear left and then turn left at a main junction. Continue on the main track past a second gate. At a T-junction turn right downhill, following this track to **Moss Rd**. Cross the road, turn left under the bridge then immediate right through a safety barrier onto a footpath. Follow this path, ignoring paths to the left and right until you reach an information board for *Central Hall*. Turn hard right just beyond the board and follow the path. Fork left at the next junction. At the T-junction, with a triangle of grass, turn left and follow the path, between a fence a brick wall, until you emerge next to **St Georges Rd** opposite a roundabout.

❸ St Georges Rd to Marshbrook Way via Muxton Marsh 1.6 miles

Cross the roundabout to go straight ahead down **Bradley Rd**. Follow the road until you see **Ash Lea Drive** on the left, then take the pedestrian route to the left of the grassy bank and follow it to the T-junction at the end. Turn left and follow the road until you reach the school.

Walk straight past the school, cross the main road, turn right and then left to walk along **Church Rd**. Take the first lane on the right, walking past a mix of houses and open land. Follow this lane for a while and at a sharp left bend, turn right through the safety barrier onto a footpath. Go under the main road then shortly turn right through a kissing gate onto *Muxton Marsh*. Continue straight, using the wooden boards to cross a wet area, and walk towards a gate.

Go through the kissing gate then immediate left. Cross the stream, turn left, then keep left. Follow the main level track through the woods. Ignore footpaths on the left and right. Climb some shallow steps and turn right at the top of the slope, continue to a T-junction and turn right. Continue through the woods following the signs all the way. Descend the steep steps down to a tarmac path, turn left and follow this path all the way past the school on your left to the main road (**Marshbrook Way**).

4 Marshbrook Way to Lilleshall Hill 1.6 miles

Cross the road (**Marshbrook Way**) using the zebra crossing and follow the tarmac path until you soon reach a road (**Muxton Lane**). Turn left, then shortly turn right onto a footpath just before **Halcyon Court**. Follow the obvious path, over a stream and straight on, crossing two fields, always in the direction of the Monument on Lilleshall Hill. When you reach the road (**Lilyhurst Rd**), turn left, then right into *Lilleshall* along **Church Rd**. After some distance, turn left up the road opposite a kissing gate and a sign for the *Memorial Hall*, and follow this all the way round to just past the *Memorial Hall*. Adjacent to a grassy bank take a sharp right up a steep footpath to the base of *Lilleshall Hill*. Then turn left uphill on a footpath and climb to the *Lilleshall Monument*. From the top of Lilleshall Hill you can see The Wrekin and admire how far you've come.

To find the bus stop for the No 5 /5A service to Telford or Newport see directions on map overleaf. To walk to Newport from Lilleshall, via the **Hutchison Way**, see pages 81, 82.

MAP Stage 6 Oakengates to Lilleshall

Ordnance Survey data © Crown copyright and database right 2017

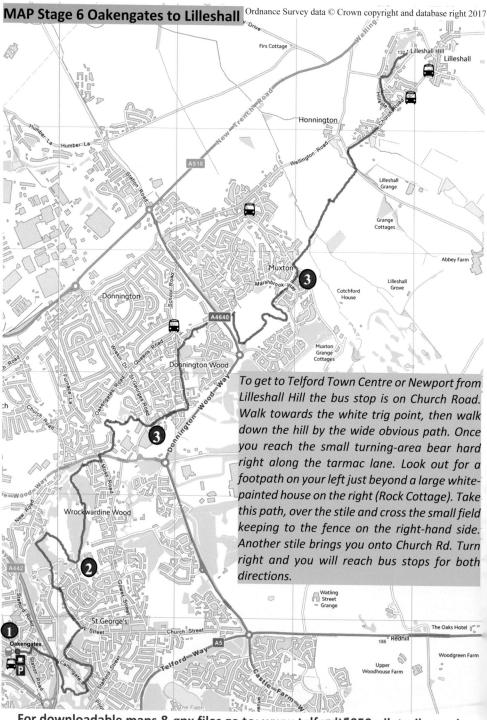

To get to Telford Town Centre or Newport from Lilleshall Hill the bus stop is on Church Road. Walk towards the white trig point, then walk down the hill by the wide obvious path. Once you reach the small turning-area bear hard right along the tarmac lane. Look out for a footpath on your left just beyond a large white-painted house on the right (Rock Cottage). Take this path, over the stile and cross the small field keeping to the fence on the right-hand side. Another stile brings you onto Church Rd. Turn right and you will reach bus stops for both directions.

For downloadable maps & gpx files go to; www.telfordt5050miletrail.org.uk

7 *This stage takes you from the lovely viewpoint of Lilleshall Hill, across fields, through Granville Country Park full of historic remnants of local industry, round the lake in Priorslee (The Flash) and into the Town Park in the centre of Telford. The No 5 bus connects Telford Centre bus station with Lilleshall.*

① Lilleshall to Granville Country Park 2 miles

f you're at the **Lilleshall Monument** walk around it and then towards the white trig point. If you've arrived by bus follow the instructions in the paragraph below from **Church Rd**). Continue down the hill by the wide obvious path. Once you reach the small urning-area bear hard right along the tarmac lane. Look out for a footpath on your left just beyond a large white-painted house on the right (**Rock Cottage**). Take this path, over he stile and through the small field keeping to the fence on the right-hand side. Another stile brings you onto **Church Rd**.

urn right and follow **Church Rd** all the way to the T-junction at the end. (If you have lready completed Stage 6 you will now be re-tracing your steps for a while). Turn left Lilyhurst Rd) and after a short distance turn right, by a gate, to join a signed footpath cross the field. Keep straight ahead, cross an area of concrete hardstanding, then cross stream. At the next stile, you depart from the stage 6 route, bear half-left diagonally cross the final field towards the centre of a thick bank of trees. This part of the trail is public footpath but may not be clear on the ground. A good stile takes you onto **Muxton** . Turn left onto the lane and continue to follow it for a while, past the golf-centre car ark on the left, until you reach a small car park on the right at the entrance to **Granville** ountry Park.

② Through Granville Country Park 1.8

Walk to the far end of the car park into the Nature Reserve. Follow the path, don't go up the steps but keep right and continue past a large derelict building (the **old winding house**). Continue to follow the main path until you reach a double gate. Go straight on past the information board for **Granville Country Park**. Just beyond the board turn left up some steps. At the top of the steps keep right.

From the top of the hill you can see the Berwyn Hills on a fine day. Continue straight ahead and drop down, via steps, to the car park. Emerge onto a road, cross it and turn right for a short distance, then turn left through the gate at the **Granville LNR** information board. Walk along the main path past the **owl sculpture** and then turn left to view the **canal basin**. Continue to follow the path beside the canal basin to re-join the main path. Turn right and immediate left down a narrow footpath to see the **Old Lodge Furnaces**. Walk past the information board and carry on, to re-join the main path again. Turn right and continue to follow the main path passing a pool on your right. Carry straight on and pass through a kissing gate. On reaching an open area you need to bear right: either follow a well-trodden narrow p: through the grass and trees or join the concrete track which runs from left to right in fr of you along the edge of the reserve. This area can get wet and muddy at times her the options. When you reach a junction of paths keep to the right, following the m straight track through a cutting (muddy at times) for about 400 yards. Then take a narr footpath that bears left through birch trees. You emerge onto a major track. Walk acr it and up through the grass to turn left on the raised tarmac path on the far side.

③ From Granville Country Park to Priorslee Lake 1 mile

Follow this tarmac path, up steps and across the bridge over the road. More steps ta you up to a more open area. Walk straight ahead, down steps at the far end, then some broad shallow steps. Carry straight on with a sports pitch on your left. There : good views back to Lilleshall Hill from here. At the corner of the sports pitch you emerge into an open area for car parking. Turn right here along a wide obvious footpa Take the first left turn through a kissing gate. Follow this path, pass through a secc kissing gate onto a wider track. Turn left onto a lane and immediate left again, at t **Cottage Spring** pub, onto the main road (**Church St**).

Continue down **Church St** and turn right, just before the church, onto **Snow Hill**. Continue straight at the crossroads into **Ashley Rd**. As this road bends to the right, bear left onto a footpath and go down the steps through the underpass towards *Priorslee Lake*.

4 Priorslee Lake to Telford Town Park via Randlay Wood 2.9 miles

Ahead of you is *Priorslee Lake (The Flash)*. Bear left where the paths fork. Carry on keeping the lake on your right, past green picnic tables, across two long bridges and then turn left on a path just before the steps. Follow this path through trees until you reach the rear of a school. Continue bearing round slightly to the right and eventually emerge onto a main road (*Priorslee Ave*). Cross the road and turn right. Stay on this road until you turn left along a road called **Priorslee Village** (there was a *clocktower* here, due to be replaced soon). Follow Priorslee Village Rd through the *old village of Priorslee*, eventually reaching a main road (**Shifnal Rd**).

Cross Shifnal Rd and turn right. After a short while turn left down a well-marked footpath following the **NCN55**. Follow this path over the motorway. Continue straight until you reach a fork in the path, keep left, crossing over a road, a railway line and another road. Bear right across the grassy open area (just before the underpass) and arrive at the junction of **Dinchope Drive** and a main road (**Dale Acre Way**). Turn right onto the main road and follow it until you reach **Downemead** on the left. Follow Downemead to the end bearing slightly left to walk in front of the shops. Continue to the main road, cross at the pedestrian crossing and turn left. Then bear right to follow the tarmac path alongside *Hollinswood School*.

Continue to follow the tarmac path, with the school on your right and a playing field on your left, go through the underpass into *Randlay Wood*. After a few yards the path splits, take the right fork. At a second split, by a metal picnic bench, again take the right fork. Continue through an open area, then woods, go through the underpass and into *Telford Town Park*. As you go through the Park gates, take the path on the immediate right. Continue straight ahead keeping a pool on your left. Ignore a footpath joining from your right. Turn right at a T-junction, pass the entrance to *Wonderland* on the left. Turn left when you reach the open grassy area and pass an adventure play area on the left to reach picnic tables in front of the remains of a ruined *Norman chapel*. **This is the end of the T50 50 Mile Trail.** There are toilets in the *Information Centre* behind the chapel. The *shopping centre*, *bus station* and *railway station* are signed and can all be reached easily from here.

This stage is well served by the No 5 bus service Telford Bus Station via Oakengates, Muxton, Donnington (5A), Lilleshall. Buses continue to Church Aston, Newport and Stafford. St Georges and Priorslee also have frequent buses to the Town Centre. Buses run every few minutes between the bus and rail stations. There are a number of car parks surrounding Telford Town Centre (pay on exit).

This trail was developed by volunteers formed from a consortium of local walking groups.

Grants from Telford T50 Fund & EnviroGrant Veolia in partnership with Telford & Wrekin Council's Pride in the Community Programme enabled the trail to be waymarked and supported.

MAP Stage 7 Lilleshall to Telford Town Park
Contains Ordnance Survey data © Crown copyright and database right 2017

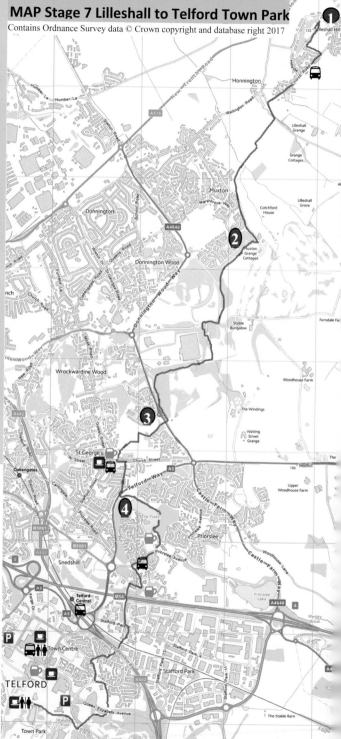

Newport is an interesting old market town, founded in the C12th, with historic buildings and the remains of a canal. From here you can walk as far as Stafford on the Millennium Way, returning to Telford via Newport and Lilleshall on the No 5 bus. To explore Newport continue down High St, then return to the Stafford St Car Park.

In Lilleshall, continue north up **Church Road** then **Limekiln Lane** and turn right into **Willmoor Lane**. After about 300 yards turn left at the fingerpost on to the *Hutchison Way* (waymarked). Continue along the disused canal towards a farm. Keep to the left side of the hard standing and turn left up a narrow path alongside the first farm building and onto the farm access road. Go through the kissing gate almost opposite and enter the woodland full of old quarries and limekilns. Continue straight along the path and ignore a path on the left. Continue straight, then down the slope. Cross the boardwalk and up through the trees to a track and kissing gate. Keep right through the kissing gate. Cross a stream and turn left to follow the field edge to a kissing gate to the **A518.** Turn right. When you reach the roundabout turn right into **Pitchcroft Lane**. Follow the lane for ¾ mile until you reach the top of a rise. Turn left through a metal kissing gate, cross the tarmac farm road and follow the footpath northwards approximately half way between the two poles, until it joins a track. Turn left and cross over the main **A518.** Take the footpath into the trees and bear immediately right. Go through a kissing gate and follow the path alongside the hedge on the left. Continue along the grassy track across the field and bear right at the fork. Go through a metal kissing gate and follow the fenced footpath around the side of the field. Keep right and walk to the road. Turn left and walk towards the centre of Newport along **Station Rd**. After about 750 yards turn right through a **covered alley**, *signed for Waitrose*, into *Stafford Street Car Park* and the *bus stands* for Telford, to Stafford, or Shrewsbury.

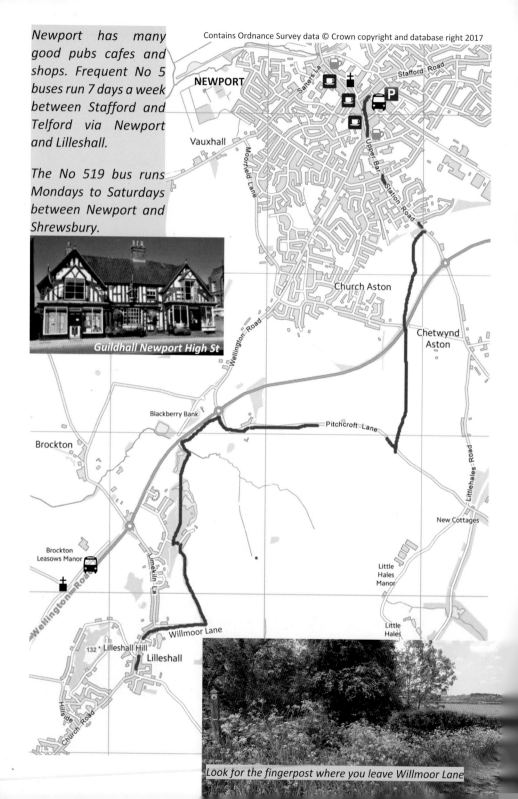

Newport has many good pubs cafes and shops. Frequent No 5 buses run 7 days a week between Stafford and Telford via Newport and Lilleshall.

The No 519 bus runs Mondays to Saturdays between Newport and Shrewsbury.

Guildhall Newport High St

Contains Ordnance Survey data © Crown copyright and database right 2017

NEWPORT

Vauxhall

Salters La

Stafford Road

Upper Bar

Station Road

Moorfield Lane

Church Aston

Chetwynd Aston

Wellington Road

Blackberry Bank

Pitchcroft Lane

Littlehales Road

Brockton

New Cottages

Little Hales Manor

Brockton Leasows Manor

Limekiln La

Little Hales

Wellington Road

Willmoor Lane

132 · Lilleshall Hill

Lilleshall

Hillside Road

Church Road

Look for the fingerpost where you leave Willmoor Lane